Little Known Tales from Oregon History

A Collection of 28 Stories from
Cascades East Magazine

VOLUME I

CASCADES EAST

Oregon's Sun-filled Mountain and Desert Playground

Published by
SUN PUBLISHING
716 NE 4th Street
Bend, Oregon 97701

Geoff Hill - Publisher/Editor

Library of Congress Catalog
Card Number: 88-90788

ISBN 0-929084-00-4

Second Printing: 1993

Foreword

The collection of *Little Known Tales from Oregon History* that make up this first volume have been reprinted from the pages of Sun Publishing's *Cascades East* magazine. The stories in this book were originally published from 1976 to 1981; a second volume will follow consisting of stories from 1982 to 1989.

The idea for a feature on history in each issue of *Cascades East* came from George W. Linn, the first editor of the magazine. He felt Oregon, and Central Oregon in particular, was rich in pioneer history that, for the most part, had never been shared in printed form. He was right.

George made numerous contacts to trace leads to the stories. Some he wrote after visiting with the person, others were published as they were written by the story teller, such as, Dean Hollinshead's "Driving Lumber Down the Deschutes on Rafts" and "As I Remember Silver Lake Days"; others were submitted by freelance writers.

There are stories of individuals, families, events, achievements, conflicts, and unsolved mysteries. Illustrated with over 100 pictures and drawings. *Little Known Tales from Oregon History* will keep the memories of the past alive for years to come.

Table of Contents

Acknowledgements

It would be easy to fill several pages about all the contributors to this book, if we were to go into detail, but let's use the pages to share more of their stories.

There are 28 stories, and over 100 photos and illustrations included in this volume, which is primarily the work of 20 different authors. We thank each and every one of them.

Special thanks to those who participated in the interviews necessary to complete many of the stories, and to the family members who gathered information and photos.

Although several of the authors are now deceased...William L. Van Allen, Frederick Arpke, Art Chipman, Ed Dyer, Dean Hollinshead, and Barney Wall...their stories will live on, and we are forever grateful.

Dedication

My wife Vicki and I dedicate this book to George W. Linn of Madras. His leadership and editorial formatting as *Cascades East* magazine's first editor, helped tremendously in the magazine's success. His idea of including a *Little Known Tales from Oregon History* feature in each issue ultimately led to the production of this book. Thank you, George!

Little Known Tales
from Oregon History

Little Known Tales from Oregon History

No. 1

A Flight to Freedom

Maggie Wewa

By George W. Linn

MAGGIE WEWA was born on the Warm Springs Indian Reservation in 1882. At 94, Maggie is one of the oldest Paiute Indians in Oregon. Far from being content to spend her golden years in a rocking chair, she spends a good portion of her time traveling to Eastern Oregon and Northern Nevada visiting relatives and participating in powwows. Her eyes are keen and twinkle merrily with an inborn wit. When she laughs — which is frequently — she laughs all over her ample frame.

Most of Maggie's travels are in the company of her grandson, Wilson Wewa, who is the 1976 prototype of the noble Indian. Standing almost six and a half feet tall, with waist-length, braided hair, Wilson carries himself with a dignity and poise that belies his youth. At 20, he is rapidly becoming a religious and cultural leader among the Warm Springs Paiutes.

During a recent visit to The White Buffalo Indian Museum in Sisters, he and Maggie related an early-day tale of Indian life that gives us a brief glimpse into a little-known, seldom-explored facet of our state's history.

Around the middle of the last century, Simtustus was the chief of the Warm Springs Indians. When a group of Paiutes visited Warm Springs, he saw a young Paiute maiden and became completely infatuated with her. Following the Indian custom, he approached the maiden's father and asked for the girl's hand in marriage, which was granted in exchange for 18 horses. And, within a year or so, a son was born to them.

Although she enjoyed high status as Simtustus' wife, the young mother was not happy. She longed for her family and friends and for the high desert country to the south and east, the vast expanse of land between the present-day cities of Bend and Burns formerly roamed by the Paiutes. So she set in motion an ingenious escape plan.

Her daily chore was the gathering of wood for the campfire. Early each morning, she would strap her infant son into his cradle board and head south toward the Metolius River. Before leaving camp each morning, she secreted a small amount of food in her clothing. She hid these small parcels of food in carefully selected caches, each one farther away from Warm Springs, each one in a straight line toward the Metolius. Each day, she made certain that she returned to Warm Springs with her quota of wood to avoid suspicion.

On the fateful day when she planned her flight to freedom, she left camp, as usual, with her infant son. Hurrying to her first food cache, she retrieved the hidden rations and continued southward as fast as the rough terrain allowed. Her only stops were at her hidden stocks of food. By the time she was out of her normal wood-gathering range, she had built up a food supply sufficient to last several days in case she had difficulty locating a band of friendly Paiutes.

Her initial destination was a Paiute campsite on Squaw Creek, just north of the present-day site of Sisters. But, in order to reach it, she would have to cross the Metolius.

She reached the Metolius north of the present site of Camp Sherman in the middle of the night. When she tested the icy water, she realized that her infant son would perish if she stumbled and dropped him while wading across the river. So she constructed a raft of reeds and floated him, "Moses style," across the watery barrier.

When she reached the Squaw Creek campsite, she found no friendly Paiutes; so she continued on, fording the Deschutes River in the same manner in which she had crossed the Metolius.

After several days of wandering, she finally encountered a friendly band of Paiutes near the present site of Millican and was returned to her family.

Not long afterward, Chief Simtustus wrote himself into the history books when he signed the Treaty of 1855 creating the Confederated Tribes of the Warm Springs Indian Reservation. Lake Simtustus, just west of Madras, bears his name. The reservation population, made up largely of Warm Springs, Wasco and Paiute Indians, has prospered and become one of the nation's most progressive Indian tribal units. His grandson, Amos Simtustus, is one of three chiefs on the reservation today. He lives at Simnasho, a tiny Indian village just a few miles north and west of Kah-Nee-Ta, the multi-million-dollar resort owned and operated by the Confederated Tribes.

The infant son of the fleeing Paiute girl grew to manhood and settled on the Warm Springs Reservation. His daughter is Maggie Wewa, a 94-year-old matriarch of the Warm Springs Paiutes. His great grandson, Wilson Wewa, who is also the great great grandson of Chief Simtustus, is destined to become a leader among his people.

Little Known Tales from Oregon History

No. 2
Dangerous Encounter

By Ed Dyer

LAW AND ORDER were slow in coming to communities East of the Cascades. Burns, some 130 miles east of Bend, was no exception. As late as 1896 or 1897, Burns was averaging three or four killings a week, and this was compounded by one major problem — there was no casket-builder in Burns. My great grandfather, George Harvey Dyer, became the casket-builder for Burns; and therein lies the tale which I call "Dangerous Encounter."

George Harvey Dyer was no stranger to violence. Born in Arkansas, he was conscripted into the Confederate Army at the age of 15 along with his brother who was only 14. They went into battle and were captured by Union forces and thrown into a concentration camp where they were systematically tortured. They were advised that the only way they could avoid the torture was to enlist in the Union Army and fight on the side of the North, which they did for the balance of the war.

When they returned to Arkansas at the end of the war, they were considered turncoats and shunned by the loyal Southerners. A short time later, a group of local citizens (probably following a visit to the neighborhood saloon) decided to "teach the turncoats a lesson." They descended on the house while my great grandfather and his father were away. The younger brother was roped and

dragged to death behind a horse. When the father returned, he took the law into his own hands and systematically hunted and killed every member of the lynch mob. My great grandfather moved to Oregon a short time later and settled in Woodburn in the Valley.

My great grandmother died in 1896 or 1897, leaving Grandpa with six children — three boys and three girls ranging in age from three to ten. It was then that he heard about Burns' need for a casket builder. So he set out toward Burns in the fall of the year, with his six children.

Even today, the McKenzie Pass is no picnic in the fall. Anytime after Labor Day, a blizzard can hit without warning. But, 80 years ago, it was even more treacherous. The road was little more than a wagon trail — steep, winding and deeply cut with ruts. As luck would have it, a blizzard did hit just as Grandpa reached the most difficult portion of the road. His team of horses was floundering in the deepening snow drifts, and it was becoming obvious that their chances of getting through the pass were slim. It was a "life or death" situation, and Grandpa knew it.

Suddenly, out of the blinding white of the swirling snow, there appeared three figures on horseback. Grandpa's spirits rose. Here was the help he had been praying for.

As they approached through the snowstorm, he got a better look at them. They were dressed for traveling, heavy jackets drawn up tight beneath their chins. Hats were pulled down low over their faces. It wasn't until they reined up alongside the wagon seat that Grandpa saw their weapons. Each saddle sheath held a well-worn carbine. Each rider wore at least one pistol strapped to his thigh in the manner of a professional gunfighter. Grandpa fought back a sinking feeling in his stomach.

"Highwaymen!" he thought to himself.

Grandpa knew that highwaymen frequented the McKenzie Pass area, just waiting for such a situation as he found himself in. The canyons below the road were littered with the remains of wagons which had been pushed over the side after the occupants had been brutally murdered by the highwaymen. He knew better than to expect mercy, but he figured that his only chance was to ignore the riders' profession.

"Hello," he called. "You're a sight for sore eyes."

No reply.

"We're on our way to Burns. My six kids are in the wagon. Their ma died, so we just packed up and left."

Still no reply. But Grandpa was determined to keep talking.

"I been praying somebody would come along to give us a hitch over the pass. You're sure the answer to my prayers."

Silence...dead silence. Grandpa climbed down from the wagon seat.

"Now, if you'll just hitch your ropes onto the wagon, we can pull'er up over the pass," Grandpa said. "It ain't more than a quarter of a mile."

Still not a word. Grandpa looked from one face to the other. It was obvious that the one in the center was the leader, so Grandpa looked him straight in the eye. The silence was deafening.

After what seemed an eternity, the leader looked at each of his confederates and nodded. Not a word was spoken as each took his lariat off his saddle and hitched onto the wagon. Grandpa jumped back onto the wagon seat.

The horses strained as the ropes grew taut. Grandpa's horsewhip cracked over his team's heads. In just the few minutes the wagon had been sitting, the wheels had frozen to the ground. Then, very reluctantly, the ice gave way; and the wagon wheels made a quarter-turn . . . then a half-turn . . . and, finally, a full turn. Once the wagon began moving, the riders kept its momentum going until it reached the downgrade at the summit of the pass. Without a word, the three removed their lariats and coiled them.

"Thank you," Grandpa said simply. "We'd never have made it without your help. God will bless you for this."

The leader looked at Grandpa.

"Yeah," he said. "I guess you're pretty lucky. Good luck in Burns."

Without another word — and without a smile — the three highwaymen turned their horses and disappeared back over the pass into the snowstorm.

Grandpa made his way to Burns and was the town's only casket-builder for several years. When law and order did reach Burns shortly after the turn of the century, the casket building business dropped off drastically; and Grandpa moved to Klamath Falls and, finally, to Cottage Grove. He died in the Veteran's Hospital at Roseburg.

Mrs. Dorothy Brasel Vandevert, 1976 (right)

No. 3

Homesteading on the Deschutes

By George W. Linn

WHEN young Dorothy Brasel made her first trip west from Chicago in 1924 to visit her uncle, Chester Catlow, near Bend, one of the young men she met was Thomas William (Bill) Vandevert. He was the only unmarried son of William P. Vandevert who had homesteaded on the Deschutes River just south of the present-day site of Sunriver some 35 years earlier.

She returned to Chicago and worked for a year before coming back to Central Oregon for another visit. She subsequently went to Portland where she worked in a bank during part of 1926 and 1927 before returning to the ranch to marry Bill.

They moved to a ranch just west of U.S. 97 on Paulina Prairie where they lived until 1935 when short water forced them to sell and move to Tumalo. They moved east of Bend in 1945, and she went to work at St. Charles Hospital in 1947 or 1948. They moved into Bend in 1959. She retired in 1969 and still lives in Bend. Her husband, Bill, passed away in 1969.

A recent visit in her home resulted in a collection of stories spanning over 100 years of Oregon history and the interesting photos on these pages, some of which go back into the early 1880's.

The stories begin with her husband's grandfather, Jackson Vandevert, who was born in Iowa and moved to Oregon City where he spent several years serving as a scout for immigrant trains coming into the Oregon country. When he heard of a wagon train approaching, he would load pack mules with bacon, flour and salt in Oregon City and head southwest to meet the incoming immi-

grants at Willamette Pass. The trip across the country took months; and, in many cases, their supplies would be exhausted and they would be practically starved. He would then guide them into the Willamette Valley.

Jackson's wife — and the mother of William P. Vandevert — was Grace Clark whose story has been written many times inasmuch as her family were the victims of the Clark massacre on the Snake River.

William P. Vandevert was born in 1854 at Oregon City. As a young man, he left home and went to Texas where he worked with the Hash Knife Outfit which Zane Grey made famous in a novel published in the 1920's. William was with the Hash Knife Outfit during the range wars fictionized by Grey. He subsequently moved to Arizona, but Indian wars made him fearful for his family; so they moved to New York for a time before returning to Oregon in 1891 when William and his family spent the winter with his father, Jackson, who had home-

The Vandevert family (left) in about 1883 (left to right): Sadie, the mother (standing), Mittye who was sent to school in New York when the family homesteaded in Central Oregon in 1892, Maude, Bill who married Dorothy in 1927, and the father, William P. Vandevert (seated).

A class picture (opposite above) in the early 1890's, including six Vandevert children. Two Vandevert girls are readily identified: Maude on the far left and Grace in the white dress. There were five Vandevert boys, but only four are in this photo; and similarity in ages makes positive identification impossible.

steaded near Powell Butte.

In the spring of 1892, William made the decision to homestead on the Deschutes River, some 20 miles south of the present-day location of Bend which did not exist at that time. Only one of William's seven children, Mittye, was considered to be of school age; and she had been left in New York to live with an aunt.

At the time of the move from Powell Butte to the Deschutes, Bill — Dorothy's husband — was about ten years old. He remembered the trip, because he rode a pony and led the family cow. They stopped at Lava Butte for lunch; and, even though it was May 1, Bill remembered the youngsters playing in the snow.

William homesteaded 160 acres and purchased the adjoining 160 acres which had a cabin on it. However, the law required that the homesteader live on the homesteaded land. As luck would have it, the cabin on the adjoining 160 acres was built right on the property line; so William simply built an additional bedroom onto the cabin —across the property line — so that he could "sleep on his homestead" as the law required.

Down through the years, numerous additions and changes were made in the original cabin; but it still stands behind the new ranchhouse which was built about 20 years ago.

School was no small problem in those days. Snow, during the winter months, was too deep for the youngsters; so the "school year" began in late May and ran until early fall.

In those days, of course, school meant the primary grades. There were no secondary schools in Central Oregon. By the time Bill reached high school age, Bend was little more than a tiny village — with no high school. So he went to Salem to attend Willamette University which did offer high school for students from the vast reaches of the Oregon frontier.

At one time, the schoolhouse was on the present-day Sunriver property — opposite the location of the Great Hall. It was later moved to a place called Harper — possibly near the present location of Harper Bridge. Much later, the schoolhouse was moved to the corner of the Vandevert Ranch property, and this building still stands today.

Later, after the city of Bend had established a high school and several of the Vandevert children had reached high school age, Mrs. Vandevert would move into Bend with the kids and the family cow early in the fall and spend the winter while the

The Vandevert ranch house (above right) as it is today. Although numerous additions were made, the "wing" to the left was probably the one built by William P. Vandevert across the property line so that he could prove his homestead.

Laying in the winter meat supply (right) in the fall off 1891 near Powell Butte. Eight deer were killed, and "not a pound was wasted." Jackson Vandevert is seated near the left corner of the tent. William P. Vandevert is on the extreme right. This was the year before William P. homesteaded on the Deschutes River south of Sunriver.

youngsters attended school.

Before Bend was founded, there was a stopping place called Staats about where the present Brooks logging pond is located on the Deschutes River in the edge of Bend today. For a time, there was a post office located at the Vandevert ranch house using the name, "Lava."

An interesting sidelight on the custom of cooperation between pioneer families to solve problems is illustrated in the way they got around the lack of refrigeration for keeping meat.

Keeping the meat during the winter was no problem, because Nature provided its own deep freeze. Summer was something else. The various ranches in the area took turns in butchering a beef, and the meat would be divided between all of them. In that way, each family had a relatively small amount of meat which could be kept without refrigeration until it was used. By the time that small amount was used, it would be another ranch's turn to butcher and divide.

During the winter that William and his family were at Jackson's Powell Butte homestead in 1891, Claude was born; and he spent virtually all of his life on the Vandevert Ranch south of Sunriver. In later years, William deeded the ranch to Claude. When William died in 1945, he was within one month of attaining the age of 90. Claude remained on the ranch until he died in 1975. A few years ago, the ranch was sold to Leonard Lundgren with the understanding that Claude and his wife could live there for the rest of their lives or as long as they wish. Claude's widow, Jeannie, still lives on the ranch.

In the summer of 1976 — and in years to come — countless thousands of out-of-state visitors as well as Oregonians will drive south from Bend on U.S. 97. Many of them will turn off onto Vandevert Road and go directly past the old Vandevert Ranch on their way to the Big River or Fall River Campgrounds or on their way to Crane Prairie or Wickiup Reservoir. Some will be conscious of the history of the Vandevert family ... of their struggles to settle and raise a family in this beautiful area. Others will whiz past without a thought.

Without families like the Vandeverts who had the courage to carve a home out of the wilderness, none of us would be enjoying the great recreational assets of Cascades East country as we know it today.

Perhaps the mathematics might be incorrect, but the Vandeverts represent the true bicentennial spirit. They were the pioneers who opened up this country, and we owe them much.

No. 4

101-Year Land Dispute

by George W. Linn

GOLD was discovered in California in 1849. The cry of the nation became "Westward Ho," as gold-hungry, land-hungry settlers swarmed into the Oregon Territory. The fact that, from ancestral times, the Indians of Middle Oregon as they were then called — the Walla Wallas and the Wascoes — laid claim to some ten million acres of Central and Eastern Oregon meant nothing to the oncoming hordes. If the settlers saw a piece of land they liked, they settled on it.

Gen. Joel Palmer, superintendent of Indian Affairs for the Oregon Territory, realized that bloodshed was inevitable unless some kind of agreement was reached. So he called for a council meeting with the Walla Wallas and Wascoes near The Dalles on June 23, 1855. The council lasted three days.

"White settlers are coming in even greater numbers," Gen. Palmer told the Indians. "There is nothing you or I can do to stem the tide. They will settle on your land. There will be bloodshed. Your people will die, and our people will die."

Gen. Palmer proposed to the Indians that, in exchange for most of the land which they claimed, the United States would set aside an Indian reservation into which white men could not go without permission. There was great bitterness among the Indians, but there was also an awareness of the truth of Gen. Palmer's statements. So a Treaty was signed on June 25, 1855.

In exchange for some 600,000 acres of reservation land plus other benefits, the Indians gave up title to some ten million acres of their ancestral lands. The reservation boundaries were carefully laid out, and a rough map was drawn to the satisfaction of the Indians and Gen. Palmer.

"A map of this reservation is herewith enclosed," Gen. Palmer wrote to Washington. "But as no surveys have been made in that region, it can only be approximate in accuracy."

It was 16 years later — in 1871 — when T.B. Handley made the first survey of the reservation; but, for some reason, he neither talked to the Indians nor referred to the map made by Gen. Palmer.

There was an immediate protest by the Indians. Handley had showed the northern boundary well south of the Indians' understanding and the western boundary further to the east.

Thus began a land dispute that plagued Congress and the courts for 101 years before it was finally settled in 1972.

A re-survey was authorized by Congress in 1886; and, in 1887, John A. McQuinn completed the new survey which agreed with the Indians' understanding. The Commissioner of Indian Affairs approved the McQuinn survey, and the disputed land became known as "The McQuinn Strip."

Pressure from whites who had settled in the McQuinn Strip brought about the formation of a Commission to study the dispute in 1890. It recommended the original Handley line which was adopted in 1894 by Congress. But that didn't end the protests by the Indians.

In 1917, Congress authorized still another study, to be made by French Mensch, U.S. surveyor, who agreed with the McQuinn survey. Because of the number of settlers in the northern

Warm Springs
Indian Reservation

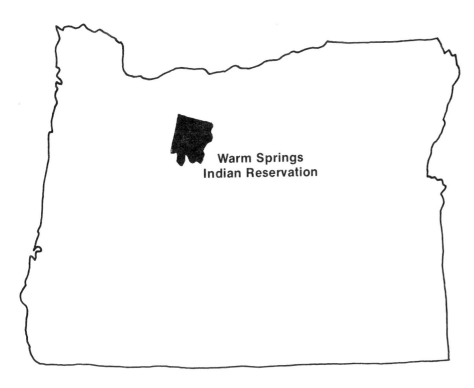

Warm Springs
Indian Reservation

McQUINN STRIP DISPUTE 1871-1972

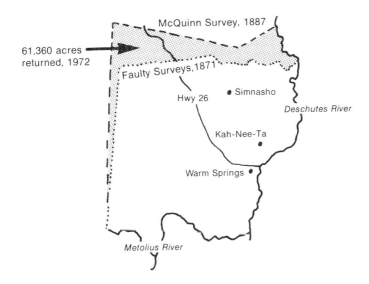

McQuinn Survey, 1887

61,360 acres
returned, 1972

Faulty Surveys, 1871

Hwy 26 • Simnasho

Deschutes River

Kah-Nee-Ta •

Warm Springs •

Metolius River

portion of the McQuinn Strip, he proposed a cash payment to the Indians for the land. The Indians refused. They wanted the land.

Congress, in 1930. authorized the Indians to take their case to the U.S. Court of Claims which, in 1941, accepted the McQuinn line except for an area of some 8,000 acres at the northeast corner of the strip. The court proposed a cash settlement based on 1855 land values of $80,925 for 80,000 acres plus interest for a total of $241,084. But, the court continued, the government had spent $252,089 in the Indians behalf since 1855; *so the Indians would actually owe the government money.*

In 1943, a bill to establish the McQuinn line was introduced in Congress. It was opposed by the Departments of Justice and Agriculture, and it failed to pass.

A measure of economic justice was achieved in 1948 when a bill passed in Congress giving the Confederated Tribes the gross revenues from the lands in the McQuinn Strip. Through 1970 this amounted to $5.95 million.

The Tribal Council, however, still held out for ownership of the land they believed was rightfully theirs even though it would have meant an actual loss of money.

The beginning of the end of the McQuinn Strip controversy began on December 8, 1971, when Congressman Al Ullman introduced a bill giving the Tribe ownership.

In the meantime, the Senate Interior Committee on July 19 approved an identical McQuinn Strip bill which had been introduced by Senators Mark Hatfield and Bob Packwood. The House Interior Committee approved it on July 26. The full Senate approved the bill on August 2, and the House followed suit on September 7. It was signed into law by President Nixon on September 21 — bringing to a close a 101-year land dispute, and giving the Indians title to most of the land which had been rightfully theirs since the Treaty of 1855.

Fearing that one 11,600-acre unit of privately-owned grazing land in the McQuinn Strip might fall into the hands of developers, the Confederated Tribes purchased it in 1971 for $40 an acre. An additional 9,000 acres in the strip and in the original reservation remain in private ownership, and the Tribes have offered to buy it from the owners. The Tribes respect the rights of those who do not choose to sell, and general jurisdiction is in the hands of the Tribal Council.

As Rep. Al Ullman said, "It took all these years to give back to the Indians land that is and always has been theirs."

Little Known Tales from Oregon History

No. 5

When the Cossacks "Invaded" Eastern Oregon

By Barney Wall

Barney Wall — lifetime Gold Card member of the Professional Rodeo Cowboys Association, Hollywood stunt rider, member of the English Polo Hall of Fame and construction man — is now retired and makes his home in Bend.

OF ALL the horsemen in both fact and fiction, none have the reputation of the fabled Russian Cossacks. All of us have read stories and seen movies dramatizing their amazing horsemanship and love for horses. It was this love for spirited horses that brought a small group of Cossacks to Eastern Oregon in 1927. They were here to buy wild horses which were rounded up in Washington, Oregon, California, Idaho, Montana and Wyoming.

Here in Central and Eastern Oregon, there were something like 35 to 40,000 wild horses roaming the desert in bands ranging in size from 10 to 50. By the early 1920's, they were a real problem. If a mare caught a wild stallion's fancy, he would simply cut her out of the rancher's herd; and she would become a part of his wild band. They ate the grass so desperately needed for cattle. They demolished fences and harrassed the ranchers. So, in the early 1920's, there were several big drives to catch them and put them to good use.

Some of these wild horses were descendants of horses brought to California by the Spaniards. Some were from the Indians — especially the Nez Perce following Chief Joseph's defeat in the late 1870's. Others had very fine blood lines, their ancestors having been brought by settlers from the blue grass country of the South. Many of them were wild as a result of the blizzard of May 1919 which swept out of Canada and down through the plains country as far south as Oklahoma and Texas.

That 1919 blizzard was a real bearcat. It probably killed as many cattle as any other storm in my recollection, and I was born in North Dakota in 1906 and lived in Alberta, Canada until I was 19 years old.

Some ranchers lost almost all their cattle. But the horses fared a lot better. You see, a horse is like a buffalo. If snow covers the grass, he paws down through it until he finds feed. If he doesn't find any, he moves on until he does. By the time many of these ranchers had dug themselves out of the snow, their herds of horses had completely disappeared. Many of them had gone wild.

As I said earlier, I was born in North Dakota and grew up in Canada. I left Canada in 1925 to live with my uncle in Santa Monica, California, in order to finish school.

One of the girls in my high school class was named Mildred Mix. Since I considered myself quite a cowboy, I was more than a little interested when I learned that her father was Tom Mix; so it didn't take me long to meet him and work the conversation around to horses.

"Maybe we could use you at the studio," he suggested. "Come on down to Universal and maybe we can get you a job working with horses."

He didn't have to sell me very hard, so I went to work as a sort of combination horse wrangler and errand boy for Ginger Rogers. I didn't have too much interest in acting, but the studio found that I was pretty good at playing a dead Indian. I did take a swing at stunt riding in two movies — "The Texan" and "Under the Tonto Rim."

I rode in my first rodeo in 1926 — the Calgary Stampede. They were shooting a movie in the area, so I just naturally wandered over to watch what was going on. A cowpuncher dressed in well-worn blue jeans approached me.

"What'cha doin', cowboy?" he asked.

"Watchin' 'em make a movie," I answered.

"Want a job?"

"Sure. Doin' what?"

"See those big reflectors over there?" He pointed to a battery of big mirrors they used to reflect the sun. "We'll give you two dollars a day for moving 'em where the director or cameraman tells you."

Two dollars a day sounded pretty big when you figure that you got $20 to $25 a month for being a ranchhand.

The cowpuncher turned out to be Hoot Gibson whom I'm proud to say became a lifelong friend. He might have been a movie star, but he was one of the best riders and shooters I've ever seen anywhere. He was really something with a .45 pistol.

Tom Mix became another lifelong friend. When he was killed in that auto accident in Arizona in 1934, I dropped what I was doing and went to his funeral. Men like Tom Mix and Hoot Gibson were cowboys first and movie stars second. Nobody who knew 'em ever called 'em "Hollywood cowboys."

I rode in my last rodeo in 1941. It was at Walla Walla, and I broke my wrist when a bucking horse throwed me. I was 35 years old, and I figured that I was old enough to have more sense. But, you know, I loved the rodeos. Still do. Every photograph that I've ever seen of me on a bucking

DeVere Helfrich Photo

horse I was grinning like a boy with a five dollar bill.

It was right around that time in the mid-20's that I first heard about the wild horses in Oregon. Rube Long and quite a few Oregon cowboys had been rounding up wild horses and shipping them out. It sounded like fun, so I headed for the Abert Rim country of southeastern Oregon.

As near as I can remember, it was in 1926 or 1927 — probably 1927 — that the Russians came into Eastern Oregon to buy wild horses. And when I say wild horses, I mean *wild horses*. They wanted the meanest, wildest, most spirited critters that we could round up. And, believe me, we had 'em by the carload.

Anybody who is an admirer of horse flesh — and those Cossacks were — had to admire these horses. They were a mixture of a little bit of everything with more than a little Satan thrown in.

Stamina? You'll never see anything like it in a domestic horse. After one was broke, you could ride him 50 miles, and he still had enough meanness left to kick you in the belly at the end of the day. For one thing, I don't think I ever saw a wild horse walk. They ran, trotted or galloped all day long. And talk about going through rough country . . . I've seen one of these old ridge runners jump off a ten-foot cliff and hit the ground running without ever breaking stride.

Most of 'em we broke what we called "cowboy gentle." That means that a tough, really good rider could stay on

him and work him — providing the horse was willing. When the horse wanted to buck — which was frequently, he'd buck off the best of 'em. And it was no joke getting bucked off 20 miles from the ranchhouse.

Now, the Cossacks didn't want 'em broke — not even cowboy gentle. They wanted 'em wild and mean just like they come in off the desert. Once in a while, they'd ask us to ride one; and they'd measure the horse's worth by how high he throwed us.

There were five Russians in the party and one representative of the U.S. — from the State Department, I guess. Four of the Russians were Cossacks — in uniform. The fifth was an interpreter. Three of the Cossacks picked out the horses they wanted, and the fourth kept records.

It's funny. It's been fifty years, but the thing I remember most about the Cossacks is their boots. They were knee-high and shined like nothing you've ever seen. Their riding pants were like any Calvary officer's pants. It was summer, so they didn't wear a tunic. They were in shirtsleeves and no tie. They wore black caps.

They were all pretty short, but stocky. The tallest wasn't over five foot ten, and they all weighed around 180 pounds. Another thing I remember is how they walked — like they had springs in their boots. When they walked out into a corral full of those wild horses, they did it without a trace of fear. They were in command, and the horses knew it. The one thing I regret is that I never got to see one of 'em

ride. That would've been worth it. You just knew that they were horsemen by the way they handled themselves.

The corral where the Cossacks picked out their horses was somewhere around Vale — I just don't remember exactly where. Anyway, they were loaded onto rail cars and sent to Portland for shipping. I understand that they also picked out some wild horses in Washington and Montana. I'm not sure how many they got, but I've heard that one shipload of 350 went out of Portland. I don't know how many more there were.

I do remember that the Cossacks' preferences ran to chunky bays and some blacks and whites. No buckskins. No Appaloosas. The one time that they failed to follow this was on a strawberry roan who was a mixture of every breed on the desert — with more than a little Devil thrown in. Anyway, those Cossacks fell in love with that widow-maker. They took him. If you're ever in Russia and see a red horse, chances are he's a descendant of that son of Satan. But watch 'im. He'll probably try to take a bite out of your arm if you give him a chance.

The Cossacks selected mostly mares. I figure they wanted to use 'em for breeding stock. They tell me that it took a year without work before the Russians would start to break the wild horses. It took that long for 'em to accustom themselves to the severe Russian climate.

Yessir, those Cossacks knew horses. Make no bones about it. They picked out nothing but the best. The ones they got had spirit to spare, but they had the makin's of great saddle horses.

For my money, there ain't no better horse on the face of the earth than a desert-bred Oregon wild horse. They run with less effort than any horse I've ever rode. They're easy to ride. You can sit in the saddle all day, because the horse does the work.

I sure wish I could paint like old Will James. If I could, there's one picture I'd paint. It would be of one of those ridge runners standing up on the horizon with his head throwed back, his nostrils flared out and just daring you to catch him.

I've seen that picture in my mind a thousand times, and I still get tears in my eyes when I think of it. Those days are pretty well gone, now. Sure, there are a few wild horses left in Central and Eastern Oregon — but not like there were 50 years ago. I guess I was the luckiest person on earth to have seen those days.

If there are any wild horses up in heaven, I'll bet old Rube Long is tryin' to catch 'em.

But, Rube, don't catch 'em all. Leave a few for me.

The Bend Water Pageant in Pictures

By William L. (Bill) Van Allen

T HE YEAR was 1933. America was just entering the Great Depression. But that didn't dim the patriotic spirit that lived in Bend. Our biggest celebration of the year was the annual Fourth of July Rodeo.

It was in that year that someone came up with the idea of a water pageant to help publicize Bend's rodeo. So the Bend Water Pageant was born — using the beautiful Deschutes River winding through downtown Bend as its stage and the majestic Cascade Range as its backdrop.

The following year — 1934 — was the first year the pageant had a queen. She was Lois Gumpert who is still active in the Bend School System.

As the years progressed, the pageant was expanded to include a parade. Then came World War II. And the Bend Water Pageant became an early casualty. The last pre-war pageant was held in 1940.

After the war, the pageant was revived in 1947; but it was never quite the same. It was continued on an "on-and-off" basis through 1965, its final year. With the demise of the Bend Water Pageant, an era of Central Oregon history came to an end — an era when community celebrations were the biggest event of the year — an era when everyone pulled together to make them a huge success.

This is, by no means, a condemnation of Bend's Fourth of July celebration as it is today. Far from it.

But there are those of us who have made Bend their home for several decades who remember the "good old days" of the Bend Water Pageant when floats in the river parade were powered by swimmers pushing from behind. We can remember some Fourth of July's when the weather refused to cooperate, and a chill wind whipped down from the snow-covered Cascades — certainly not my idea of a good day to be pushing a float down the Deschutes River.

It was on years like that the floats seemed to move a little faster as the swimmers put out a little something extra to help keep them warm.

William L. Van Allen
Weekend Photographer

History isn't always recorded with words. Since the advent of the camera, it has been used extensively to give us a pictorial history of the times. William L. (Bill) Van Allen has been doing just that for Central Oregon since 1925.

Bill was born in Buffalo, New York, in 1902. His family moved to the Pacific Northwest (the Seattle area) in 1905 — by stagecoach. In 1909, they moved to Redmond — traveling from Seattle to Shaniko by rail and from Shaniko to Redmond by stagecoach. Bill moved to Bend in 1930 where he was in the automobile business until retirement in 1962.

Although Bill describes himself as a "weekend photographer," he has one of the largest files of photographs of anyone in the area. Always a lover of the outdoors, Bill has made something of a specialty of deer photographs; and his photographs of deer alone number in the thousands.

He is the author of a novel, "The Four Seasons of Survival," which was published in 1967 and is now out of print. It is, quite naturally, illustrated with his photographs.

During the years, Bill has traveled extensively — always with his camera. If you need a photo of a herd of elephants in Africa, he has it. The same for a Tahitian bathing beauty or a street scene in Hong Kong.

Bill loves pageants and parades. Because of this interest, we are fortunate in being able to bring you this pictorial feature which is certain to bring back many memories of one of Central Oregon's most colorful pageants.

1959 Pageantarians (facing page, left). They are (left to right): Dr. Don Pence, Marion Cady, Owen Panner, Bruce Cullison, unidentified, H.A. Pyzdrowski and Glen Gregg (deceased).

Mrs. Len Standifer was the chaperon and is seated in front of the Queen and her Court in an undetermined year (facing page, right). The editor regrets that identification of the girls is missing. If you recognize any of them, please let us know; and we will publish their names in the Summer issue.

1959 Queen and her Court (above, left to right): Pat Feeney; Joan Benson (Mrs. Bill Wheeler); Susan Moore (Mrs. Gary Van Uitert); Queen Pat Hollenbeck (Mrs. Dale Moyer); and Judy Haines (Mrs. Phil Hatch). Pilot Butte Inn is in the background.

1962 arch through which parade of floats came (above right). This was the year the arch caught fire. A passing teen-ager shed his clothing, swam out to the arch and extinguished the flames.

1954 float which carried the Queen and her court (right). Swans in the foreground are genuine.

1958 arch (below) with floats lined up in the lower right portion of photo.

1960 parade through downtown Bend (below right).

William L. Van Allen Photos

First photo ever made of Rim Rock Riders (above) taken on the Dean Hollinshead Ranch.

Morris Hoover and his wife (above) on the trail south of Broken Top near Green Lakes.

Lily and Dean Hollinshead (below) near Todd Lake with Mt. Bachelor in the background.

Little Known Tales from Oregon History

No. 7

40 Years with the Rim Rock Riders

THIS year - 1977 - marks the 40th anniversary of the group of Central Oregon horse lovers known as the Rim Rock Riders. My wife, Lily, and I have been a part of this group from the very beginning - even before it was known as the Rim Rock Riders. And, believe me, we've packed a lot of good times and made a lot of good friends in this 40 years.

It all began in the spring of 1937. None of us had any idea that our Sunday afternoon rides would develop into a permanent organization. But it did.

In the beginning, there wasn't more than 10 or 15 of us. We had three things in common. We loved horses. We loved to ride. And all of us lived in and around Bend.

Just about any Sunday afternoon, we'd get together and head up into the hills or out into the desert - on horseback, of course. We had some great times, and the word began to spread; so had more and more riders almost every weekend.

One Sunday when Lily and I knew the riders were going to Shevlin Park, we "cooked up" a surprise for them. We took our car and drove to the park. When the riders arrived, we had a buckaroo breakfast cooked for the dozen or so riders. We didn't know it at the time, but this was destined to be the first of many, many trail breakfasts down through the years. And it was also on this Sunday that we began to plan for bigger and better things for the riding group.

The next thing we knew, Jack Meford and his wife invited the whole bunch to their place for a get-together in the evening. That's when the riding club began to take shape. Before the evening was over, we had elected a president, a secretary and all the "goodies" that it takes to form a pleasure group. I'm not sure, but I think the name, Rim Rock Riders, also came into being that night

I don't remember all the people who were there that night, but they were the back bone of the Rim Rock Riders which has lasted 40 years and is still going strong. Some that I know were Jack Meford and his wife, Sergeant Lowel Hirtzel and his wife, Les Dodson and his daughter, Eve, Rube Long, Shorty Gustafson, Frank Filey

Lily Hollinshead on "Rainy Weather."

Lily Hollinshead, Clarence Calvin and Dean Hollinshead (above) eating lunch near the head of Tumalo Creek.

and his wife, Rod Rosebrook and, of course, me and Lily as well as some I'm sure I've forgotten.

But I will say that these are the people who put the Rim Rock Riders together and kept the group going for all these years. Some of them are gone. But, wherever they are, I'll bet they have many pleasant thoughts about the good times (and bad times) we had - and still do.

As time went on, the Rim Rock Riders ran into that thing called progress. Our club growed so fast that we needed some place to meet other than at someone's house.

About that time - just before World War II - the government formed a sort of "home guard with horses." They needed barns for the horses, so they built a huge barn that would hold up to 50 head. (We called this barn the Big White Elephant). They used this barn for a year or so and got a lot of bills piled up against 'em - not countin' the cost of pasturing - before the people in charge found out that the government didn't have any money to pay for such things.

One of the Rim Rock Riders, Nealy Gilbert, got to poking around and found out who had money tied up in this barn. He brought it up before the club, and we decided to look into it. We found out that the debtors would be happy just to get their money back, so we bought it. That gave us lots of room for our meetings and so forth.

At that time, we were very active - especially where parades were concerned, thanks to Les Dodson who was parade chairman. He not only lined up parades for us to ride in, but

The late Lester Dodson (above), one of the original Rim Rock Riders.

Dean Hollinshead's pure palomino, "Mac" (below), veteran of nine movies.

Lily Hollinshead, Keith Grover and Dean Hollinshead (below) riding a ridge near Mt. Bachelor.

he did a lot of prodding to get us to go. We would go to Madras, Prineville, Redmond and Bend. We sure had a lot of big times at those parades.

Every year about Labor Day, we had a three-day trip to Todd Lake. It was always a pretty good guess that we'd have at least one good snow storm before we got back. You could count on it. But it was fun.

In them days, horse trailers was kind of scarce. Most of us would ride that 20 miles or so to Todd Lake and none of us thought much about it. But, nowadays, just about everybody has horse trailers and campers or motor homes. Back then, all we had to sleep in was tents regardless of the weather.

I remember one trip to Todd Lake - back in '39, I think.

Lily and I wanted to ride, so Phil Coyner and his wife took my pickup and our camping equipment up ahead of us and had camp all set up. This consisted of one tent and bedding enough for five of us. Minnie Livingston was the fifth one in the party.

We got a late start from the ranch. Lily wanted to ride one of our American saddle bred mares named Blue Jean. She wasn't hardly broke for this trip.

First off, Lily's mare didn't want to go. When we got to Portland Bridge over the Deschutes River, Blue Jean decided that was as far as she was going. She stopped. So Lily and I changed horses. Lily took my horse, Mac, and my saddle with the stirrups at least six or seven inches too long for her; and I took Blue Jean whose stirrups was that much too short for me. Lily and Minnie went on across the bridge with no trouble, but that mare of Lily's refused to even set foot on the bridge.

About that time, a car pulled up behind me and eased up real close. He had one of those big old fog horns that some of us had on our cars.

"Bla-a-a- !" One blast of that fog horn was all it took. I think Blue Jean made it across the bridge in not more than four jumps and passed the other two horses as she headed on toward Todd Lake. About a mile on down the road, Lily and I traded horses again; and she had a pretty well broke horse from there on.

About five miles before we got to Todd Lake, it began to rain and snow. Believe me, we was plenty cold by the time we reached camp. Les Dodson, a real friend, give me the biggest drink of whiskey I'd ever seen. From there on, everything was sure fine as far as I was concerned. The cooks had a hot meal for us, so I just pulled the saddles off the three horses and turned 'em loose. When I woke up the next morning, Mac had his head stuck inside the tent lookin' for me. We had no trouble

rounding up the rest of the horses, even though there was six inches of snow on the ground.

Our saddles were all out in the wet. The cooks were over by the big fire gettin' breakfast. We all ate together. Everyone helped which was a good thing on a morning like that.

Walt Smead tied his horse to a small jack pine. The horse didn't seem to like that arrangement, so he pulled the tree out by its roots and ran off with tree and all. The horse ended up - upside down - in a little creek. That made it easy for Walt to catch his horse.

We all rode up toward Broken Top for about two hours before coming back to camp for lunch. We headed back toward Bend about 12:30. Gettin' back to Bend took about four hours. It was all down hill. It was nice and warm, all the snow had melted off the ground; so it was real good ridin'.

Minnie Livingston gave up on ridin' back with us, so Lily took her horse back to Bend. I led Lily's mare back for her.

As time went on and progress kept bothering us, we had to have more money to have less fun. It so happened that the cleaners and dyers had a big convention here in Bend, and they wanted the Rim Rock Riders to put on a big buckaroo breakfast for them. The fact that we didn't have any place or any equipment to do this didn't slow us down a bit. We said, "Let 'er Rip."

We counted on maybe 50 to 75 people. But you know what? We ended up by serving about 375 breakfasts. This was done at mine and Lily's Timberlane Ranch. With that many people, we needed room; and room was the one thing we had plenty of - thanks to good, old Mother Earth. The people got their food and sat wherever they could find a spot on the ground. But they loved every bit of it.

We were lookin' around for enough equipment to cook all these breakfasts. We found a couple of hotcake griddles and everything else we needed - that is, everything but stoves. Then, lo and behold, Phil Coyner come up with a big, double, wood-burning range - the kind they used in logging camps. It had two big hot plates on top and lots of room for wood. So what more could you want? Phil said he'd give me the stove if I'd come over and haul it out of his house. I was over there before he could change his mind. I brought it out to my ranch and set it up out under some big yellow pines. We were ready to go.

The cleaners and dyers must have been happy with the breakfast, and I guess the word spread. Anyway, we kept on giving big breakfasts three or four times a year for about five years or so.

Since we gave those breakfasts on my ranch, I was put in as breakfast chairman. Out of all the members of the Rim Rock Riders, I'll bet I was the only one who couldn't boil water without scorching it.

Then progress caught up with us again - for the last time, I hope. We sold the Big White Elephant barn and bought the old "Glen Vista Club" about four miles north of Bend. And that's where we still are. We have about 200 members now, and we're still goin' strong. We have a big summer camp up near Elk Lake in conjunction with the U. S. Forest Service on Quinn River. It's one of the best camps in Oregon. If I say so myself.

The Rim Rock Riders have rode most all the mountain trails. From Todd Lake up to Tom McArthur Rim and down to Green Lakes. The Skyline Trail as far south as Mink Lake. We've been out in the desert as far as Christmas Valley. We've rode Crack in the Ground and Hole in the Ground. We've stayed at Gebhardt Well. We've rode as far out as Fort Rock and back in one day. We've gone out to the Rod Rosebrook Desert Ranch. We've rode up to the old castle and helped move cattle many times. If there was anything to do on horseback, we've done it.

The Rim Rock Riders went to Rube Long's ranch at Fort Rock many times and helped move his horses.

One time, we went to Fort Rock to a dance and stayed and danced almost all night. From there, we went 16 miles to the Harrison place and then on to Rube's place where we stayed about two hours until daylight before we rode into the Devil's Garden where Rube had a big buckaroo breakfast waitin' for us. Of course, Rube couldn't have done all this by himself. If you don't believe me, call up the Redmond Saddle Club and ask them about it. They were there, too.

Most everyone had to go into the Devil's Garden by horseback, but it was possible to get a pickup into the breakfast area; so I took my pickup and made about ten trips over the lava beds haulin' everyone over there that wanted to go.

Rube used to say that there was one thing that he had lots of, and that was space. He sure did, too.

On these kinds of trips with so many people and horses, I have never seen or heard any kind of arguement that was serious. They all seemed to enjoy all these trips. It was their trip. Everyone was his own boss. Everyone furnished his own stuff; and, if he didn't have what he needed, it was his own doggone fault.

The Rim Rock Riders have been together from 1937 up to 1977. That's 40 years. And, take it from me, that's a lot of happy years.

GREAT GIFT IDEA!

The Little Known Tales you've been reading have been reprinted from the pages of *Cascades East*. A *Little Known Tales from Oregon History* feature is included in each issue of this quarterly magazine.

You're invited to subscribe...
for yourself, a relative, or friend.

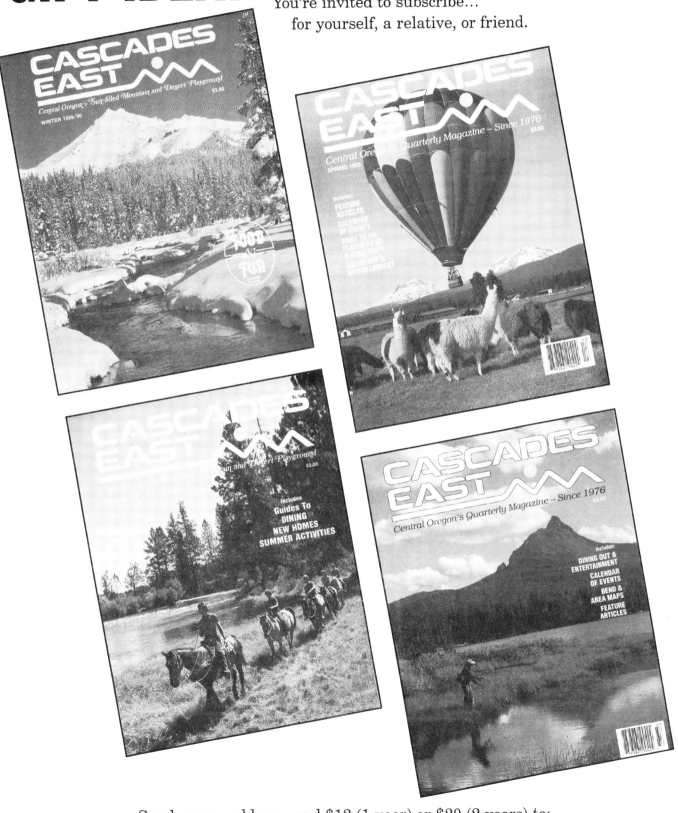

Little Known Tales from Oregon History

No. 8

In Search of the Camp Polk Site

Frederick Arpke (above) pointing out the trac[k] the old military road through Indian Ford Ranch sign (below) identifying the Squaw Creek site.
Cascades East Staff

By Frederick Arpke

Frederick Arpke, one of the co-owners of Indian Ford Ranch just north of Sisters, moved to the area in 1971 and became intrigued with pinpointing the actual site of Camp Polk. After talking to many old-timers and descendants of the original settlers, he has found a divergence of opinion and few actual facts. He agreed to author the following article with the hope that some light may be shed on the mystery surrounding the Camp Polk site.

THE STORY of Camp Polk appears simple enough. It was established as a military outpost during the campaign against the Paiute chief, Paulina, in September 1865 and operated until the spring of the following year. It is a commonly accepted fact that Camp Polk was the forerunner of the present city of Sisters. But, once we attempt to go beyond these two facts, the picture gets hazy, indeed.

For example, if Camp Polk ceased to exist as a military post in the spring of 1866 (which it did), why then does every Oregon map up through 1887 continue to show Camp Polk.

The first map which I have seen showing Sisters was published in 1900. The obvious answer, then, must be that there was a community (or, at least, a post office) known as Camp Polk as late as 1887. And, if that community was known by the name Camp Polk, doesn't it follow that it was located on the site of the military outpost? That appears to be where the confusion begins.

To put these facts into proper perspective, let's begin with the map of 1878 which was apparently published by J.K. Gill & Co. and shows only four communities in Central Oregon — Prineville, Willoughby, Warm Springs and Camp Polk. This 1878 map also shows the Willamette Valley & Cascades Military Road which ran from Sweet Home to Prineville, passing just south of Black Butte and running past Camp Polk before crossing the Deschutes River (which, on this map, was spelled Deschuttes). This military road gives us our first clue.

When I built my home on Indian Ford Ranch in 1970, I unknowingly selected a site which was directly on this old military road. The road depression, which was later pointed out to me by an old timer, is still visible.

Instead of continuing eastward to cross the Deschutes River at Tethrow Bridge, it swung about four miles south to the head of Deep Canyon — the present site of Fryrear Dump. This is well south of Highway 126 which crosses the canyon at its deepest point.

Just about a half mile south of my home on the banks of Indian Ford Creek is the site which numerous Central Oregonians (myself and Harold Barclay included) believe to be the original Camp Polk site. On the other hand, other Central Oregonians equally knowledgeable as Harold and I hold out for the site which is more

commonly accepted — on Squaw Creek.

Mrs. Aubrey Perry who grew up on the Squaw Creek Ranch says she can remember playing in the old Camp Polk barracks as a child. It is further said that, when the barracks were demolished, the lumber was used in the old barn which stands today on the Squaw Creek meadow. I am in no position to question Mrs. Perry's memory. I think it may be largely a matter of interpretation. But let me present the reasons I believe this to be the case.

From a military point of view, the Indian Ford Creek site offers much better visibility than the Squaw Creek site. I can't imagine that a military man would select the Squaw Creek site which is located down in a gulch when he was up against an

remains of the old log cabin (above) which is ~~ved by many to have been the original site of ~~p Polk. The old barn (below) which is near the ~~al cabin site.   Cascades East Staff Photos

adversary of the obvious caliber of old Chief Paulina.

There is little doubt in my mind that a "part" of Camp Polk was on the Squaw Creek site, but it's my belief that this is the location of the stables where there was a meadow and ample grass for the horses.

Indian Ford Ranch was homesteaded in the late 1860's by the Hindman family. I have never been able to verify the exact date, but it was prior to 1871 which is the date of the Indian Ford water rights. The ranch, now in Deschutes County, was in Crook County at that time. The Indian Ford water rights, which we share with Black Butte Ranch, were filed in Prineville in 1871 — the second oldest water rights in the area, being superseded only by the Enoch Cyrus water rights in 1869.

Sketches of the area made during the Williamson Army Engineer Ex-

pedition of 1855 show this portion of Indian Ford Creek as having been a dense willow thicket at that time. Why, then, would Hindman have selected such a site for his store and post office if it had not previously been cleared of willows?

The next link in the chain brings us to the 20th century.

At the time my associates and I bought the ranch in 1961, an ancient log cabin was standing on the bank of Indian Ford Creek. This was the post office, store and living quarters built by the Hindmans. Harold Barclay believes this cabin was on the original Camp Polk site. Nearby, there was the foundation of another dwelling (still visible today) and an ancient barn which is still standing. I have never been able to establish the age of the barn, but it is quite old.

More important, it had a well that was always referred to as the Military Well. It was a hand dug well which we deepened and used for several years until we went for a deeper drilled well with greater capacity.

Due to a breach of communications some years ago, the old log cabin was dismantled. I still get furious every time I think about it. Fortunately, however, the original logs were preserved; and, someday, when I can find a qualified person to do the job, I want to have the old cabin restored on its original site. I have several photographs of the log house before it was demolished, but it's going to take an expert to put the "jigsaw puzzle" together again.

The area's interesting history continued well into the 20th century.

In the early 1920's, there was talk of building a railroad from Bend to the Metolius River area to handle shipments of the timber growing on the slope of the Cascades and into the Sisters area.

During this talk about a logging railroad — in 1924 — a sizeable land purchase was made by Col. S. Orie Johnson, father of Rep. Sam Johnson of Redmond. He purchased Black Butte Ranch, the land in the vicinity of the Head of the Metolius and the Sundown and Krug Ranches on Indian Ford Creek.

Unfortunately, the railroad never became a reality. Col. Johnson sold Black Butte meadow to Stewart S. Lowery in 1936 and the timber around the meadow shortly thereafter. Lowery was a wealthy San Francisco business man who, in 1934, had purchased most of what is now Indian Ford Ranch. The Head of the Metolius — certainly one of Central Oregon's premier scenic attractions — is still owned by Rep. Johnson, but he donated the viewpoint where thousands have gazed in awe at this unusual, natural phenominon to the U.S. Forest Service some years ago.

I fully realize that this short article has not answered the question of Camp Polk's original site. But it has brought up some questions, the answers to which might prove the key to unlock the puzzle. There are several questions to which I would like to have answers.

First, in what year did the Hindman family homestead Indian Ford Ranch? That could provide a clue.

What happened to the Hindman family? Are there any survivors? I have never been able to find a single person who can tell us where the family went after leaving this area.

And, in more recent times, who or what organization is responsible for the erection of the sign identifying the Squaw Creek site as the location of Camp Polk? What was their basis for this conclusion? This sign suddenly appeared alongside Camp Polk Road some six or eight years ago, but I have never been able to find anyone who knows who erected it or on what authority.

Until some of these questions are answered, the exact location of Camp Polk will continue to be a mystery — to me and to numerous other Central Oregonians with whom I have discussed it. It is regrettable that such an important historical site should be "lost." If any reader can shed any light on any of these questions, I hope they will contact me in care of *Cascades East Magazine* or at Indian Ford Ranch, Sisters, Oregon 97759.

As I Remember
SILVER LAKE DAYS

JUSTINE Ackerson and Dean Hollinshead on one of the ice skating ponds near Silver Lake. In the background is one of the "crack-the-whip" lines.

By Dean Hollinshead

In 1925, I bought a half interest in a U.S. Mail contract from Earl Hackney and started my long mail-hauling experience. The contract was between Bend and Silver Lake.

Earl and I operated for about six months. At that time, he said he wanted to get out from under his contract; so my brother, Cecil, bought the other half interest. That gave me a new partner, and we stayed that way up until 1957 at which time I sold out my logging and went into farming.

We had two Big Six Studebakers that we ran on the mail run. One would leave Silver Lake each morning and go to Bend while the other car left Bend and went to Silver Lake. I drove one car, and Cecil drove the other. I got to Silver Lake early every other afternoon, so I had lots of time each day. It didn't take long to know everyone at Silver Lake, so we began to have fun.

In the early fall, we would go out and shoot rabbits or, sometimes, ducks and geese. We always had lots to do. There were always lots of high school kids to go with me any time, as

ENJOYING a sleigh ride near LaPine are Justine Ackerson (left) and Lily Hoard, later to become Mrs. Dean Hollinshead.

long as I furnished the car and gas.

Cecil took a contract to furnish 15 jack rabbits a day to a fox farm at LaPine. On the nights I was in Silver Lake, friends and I would try to get our quota of rabbits. There were lots of rabbits in those days. We furnished the shells, and the gang did the shooting — one driver and one shooter on each front fender. If we were lucky, we came in with jacks. After doing this for about a month, we found out we were losing money most every day, so Cecil put a stop to our fun. But we still got a few ducks and sage hens. I would take the birds to a friend of mine, and he would cook them for me; so I really had some fine feeds — along with two schoolteacher friends.

One day, just before Christmas, I went out all alone and found some birds. I got out of the car and pulled down on one. In my gun sights, I saw a paper sack under a sage brush. I didn't shoot but went to look see what it was. Six pint bottles of moonshine.

"Oh, boy," I thought. "That's pretty good." So I picked up the sack and started for the car. My toe hit something. I looked down, and there were six more pints scattered on the ground. When my toe hit the sack, it tipped over and spilled its contents on the ground. Before I left there, I had picked up six sacks, each with six pints of moonshine in them. That's 36 pints in all, and that's a lot of moonshine.

I put them in the car and went about three miles out in the desert until I came to a fence corner where I hid all of them in a big bunch of tum-

Six tobogganers aboard the "Six Foot Flex-a-Bob" on Mt. Hager. They are (left to right): Lily Hoard, Chuck Freeman, the late Sam Corum, Leonard Pitcher, Justine Ackerson and Art Harper. Standing on skis, Frank Pitcher.

TAKING a toboggan ride are (left to right): Dean Hollinshead, Lily Hoard, and Justine Ackerson.

bleweeds. When I got back to Silver Lake about dark, I went to the hotel to eat my dinner. After I ate, I went back in the kitchen to find Ed Lundy, because I knew he liked a nip once in a while.

"Ed, if you would like a drink, go out to 'such and such' a fence corner," I said. "You'll find a bottle of moonshine. You can have it if you'll go after it."

I guess Ed found it; because, when I came back the next day, everyone in town was "out" — and I do mean "out." They must have drank all of it, because I never did see any of it again.

As winter would start to creep up on us, we got lots of ice on all the big ponds around Silver Lake. We had skating ponds from ten acres up to probably 25 acres. The ice was just as smooth as glass, but the ponds were some four to five miles out of town.

Everyone around Silver Lake would rather stay home on an evening where it was nice and warm. No one thought about skating only on small ponds just over the fence. Then they didn't have to look for a ride.

But when I got there, things began to look different. By that time, we had a freight truck along with our two stage cars. We had an extra driver — Shorty Gustafson who now lives at Christmas Valley and is still going strong.

On the nights Shorty and I were in Silver Lake at the same time, we would get two or three kids and our skates and head for one of the big ponds. We had a time. So the next time, we had more kids, more grown ups, more people with cars and lots more wood for fires.

It got so everyone that had a car would load up and hit for the Walt Kitridge ice pond. We could get 25 to 30 people every time we went out.

There was one young, newly married couple who had a Model T Ford. They would come out to the pond and put their car out on the ice. They'd tie two ropes on the back bumper, and everyone would grab on. The girl would drive and the rest skate. She would crack the whip with us, and the devil take care to make you stay on the ice or you'd go out onto the dry bank. Ice skates don't work good on bare ground.

We took one brake rod loose; so, when she turned and put on the brake, the car would jack knife and that was all she wrote. No chance to stand up unless you let go and skated on your own. Out of all the days and nights we skated, I don't think anyone was hurt.

By this time, the snow began to pile up on Mt. Hager about eight miles southeast of Silver Lake. So off we went to the snow mountain.

Shorty, Frank Pitcher and Chuck Freeman made the first trip up there with skis and sleds to see what things looked like. It looked good.

That weekend, we went up for a trial run. We took everything that would slide and had a big time. But Shorty and I thought we should have a toboggan, so we got a new "Six Foot Flex-a-Bob." Then we were all fixed up. Six could ride at one time, and you could drive it just like a baby buggy. We didn't have any real fun down the hill to start with, so we had to go over logs and between trees if we were lucky.

Every time we had time, we would all go up to the big hill on Mt. Hager and have a big time. It was just like skating. Every time we went, there were always new and different cars and people. We still skated nights, but most always went to the big hill in the daytime.

I still had to work and drive stage between Silver Lake and Bend. Part time, when I met the Silver Lake Stage at LaPine, Cecil would go back to Bend, and I would go back to Silver Lake. By that time, I was pretty much interested in one of the school-teachers, Lily Hoard by name. I later changed her name to Lily Hollinshead.

Lily was from Minnesota, and something had apparently been bothering her. So one day she spoke her piece.

"I wish I could have a good sleigh ride just like I used to have when I was a young girl in Minnesota."

"All right," I said. "If you want a sleigh ride, you shall have it if you will go to LaPine and back next Saturday."

"Okay," she agreed. So I rented a team and sleigh to meet me at LaPine at noon on Saturday.

We left Silver Lake Saturday with the mail and took Justine Ackerson, a school teacher, along to go sleigh riding with us. When we got to LaPine, the team and sleigh was waiting. And away we went for about two hours.

My brother, Cecil, had to wait there until we got back; because we didn't dare leave the mail lock sacks. So Cecil stayed and guarded the four sacks.

We were about two hours late with the mail at Silver Lake, so the editor of the Silver Lake Leader put it in the paper.

"The stage was late last Saturday on account of one passenger and a heavy 'male,'" he wrote.

Yessir, we had lots of fun in those days. All the people were real good to have fun with.

LILY Hoard on skis and dressed in the ski fashions of that era.

Yessir, we had lots of fun in those days. All the people were real good to have fun with.

LILY Hoard standing in front of the Chrisman Hotel in Silver Lake before it burned.

RAMBLER with tire trouble. Claude's dad is jacking up wheel. Note the hard leather boots on tires to help get more traction and save rubber.

Claude Kelley:
PIONEER
PHOTOGRAPHER

By Jim Anderson

1920 4-cylinder Jackson (below), one of three sold in Bend that year to Hunter, Staats and Linster who owned a sawmill. Claude Kelley made this photo near Tumalo Bridge. Riders are dressed for a roller skating masquerade party.

In 1976, the computer cameras of Viking I and II gave us our first glimpse of the stark, rock-strewn surface of the red planet — Mars.

In 1907, long before computers or Vikings, a 14-year-old boy straddled a horse and started across the stark, rock-strewn sagebrush country between Wilbur, Washington and Bend, Oregon. The distance from Wilbur to Bend was over 400 miles ... but, to Claude Kelley, a pioneer, it must have seemed like the millions of miles between Earth and Mars. Claude's trip was similar to the Vikings' trip — filled with awe, excitement and the wonder of the relatively unknown

Claude was born in 1893 in the young, sputtering town of Walla Walla, Washington (that's the town everyone liked so much they named it twice). He spent his first five years there before his family moved onto a sprawling wheat ranch near Wilbur. Claude's dad ran a big wheat operation in those days. He had over 400 acres in wheat and was leaving another 320 acres of bunch grass land he planned to put into grain. Claude can remember the snail's pace speed of the single bottom, walking plow as they turned over the wild land. It took almost three years to bring the bunch grass into wheat.

At the turn of the century, America was getting restless. The Native Americans were "under control." The western part of the nation was being offered for settling in the name of "Progress."

By the time Claude was ten years old, George Eastman had made some unbelievable progress in cameras and in film processing. Photographers all over the country were seeing new technology carrying what Brady had done in the Civil War into the pages of history. Photography and land development were destined to change many things for Claude Kelley.

Claude had celebrated his 14th birthday when his father and uncle returned from a trip into the young, growing area around Bend. His father spent long hours around the kerosene lamp telling the family about the beautiful land opening up along the winding Deschutes River.

At the same time, the Cary Land Act was getting into full swing; and the dreams and claims of the land developers first appeared on the Oregon scene. Stories of towering, snow-capped mountains sparkling in the sunlight captured the imagination of many, while others could see the agricultural opportunities offered by the rich land yielding tons of

wheat and produce. Brochures and word-of-mouth carried these tales of "throbbing commerce" and "the land of plenty" to be had in Oregon, By 1907, the entire Kelley family was convinced that to stay in Washington would mean passing up the opportunity of a lifetime. Oregon Fever had struck.

On to Oregon

Going from Wilbur to Bend in 1907 was not like it is today with freeways all the way. The only vehicles using the roads in those days were horse-drawn. The big wheels of freighters and stages cut deep ruts into the native sagebrush lands. What "roads" there were could not have been called "perfect" by anyone's standards.

In July, all the family belongings were loaded into two, big freight wagons and pulled by four draft horses

the Kelley's had used for pulling the big plows in the wheat country. Those of the family not driving the wagons were loaded into a hack pulled by a two-horse team. The family also had a good buckboard which was lashed to the rear of the hack and pulled. In addition, there were 16 head of horses that the family wanted to bring along. Claude and his younger brother were given the responsibility of driving the remuda all the way.

Most of the time, the string of horses stayed pretty close; but, in the big scab land country near the Snake River crossing, it took some good cowboying to keep them going in the direction of the ferry — the only way across the Snake. All through the months of July, August and part of September, the Kelley family rolled across the Oregon country, headed for Bend. They arrived just in time for Claude to start school.

When the Kelley family arrived in Bend, they were fortunate to find someone had previously fenced a goodly portion of Awbrey Butte. Since no one was using the area, the Kelley horses were turned out to "pasture" in the lava and bitterbrush on the juniper-covered hill west of Bend.

Housing was a big problem in those days — much as it is today. Rentals were scarce, and building materials were always in great demand, coming from two small sawmills near Bend. C.A. Chapman owned a two-story house on the corner of Wall and Minnesota Streets — where the Smart Shop is today. The Kelley's moved into this building, renting both the downstairs and upstairs portions.

The Photography Bug

Claude was just getting settled into the 7th grade in Bend's all-grade

WALL Street looking south from Pilot Butte Inn location. 1904.

school located where the Deschutes County Court House Annex now stands, when the photography bug bit him. Claude's dad was in the freighting and livery business, and the family wanted a record of their activities to keep for the future. What better way to do this than with a camera? So Claude's career in photography was under way.

He looked at the cameras and supplies available and settled for a Montgomery Ward 4x5 Ansco box camera. A corner of the Kelley house was set aside as a "darkroom;" but, because of the limited light given off the kerosene lamps, the processing was carried out day and night. Nights were for developing film and days for making contact prints with the aid of sunlight. This was standard practice among early-day photographers.

It didn't take long for the "city life" to get to the Kelley clan. They were

*C*laude's dad was in the freighting and livery business, and the family wanted a record of their activities to keep for the future. What better way to do it than with a camera? So Claude's career in photography was under way.

soon on the move again, but only to the "outskirts" of town. A small, two-room, tarpaper shack was located on some acreage of a would-be homesteader's land that Claude's father purchased. With the industry of the Kelley clan, it wasn't long before a big, two-story house, barns and outbuildings were constructed. The Kelley family was here to stay.

Claude was almost 15 years old when he turned out his first photograhic print, a photo of the early Pilot Butte Canal across present-day Greenwood Avenue and the railroad tracks.

The "rules" of early irrigation plans stated that a canal would carry water into the alfalfa country until such times as the flumes that carry the water today could be constructed. Claude's photograph is a historical record of the evolution of our present-day irrigation system. In fact, it wasn't long until Claude and his $7.00 Ansco were seen throughout the Bend area carefully preserving a record for us to view today.

Enter the Rambler

Claude's uncle, H.H. Davies, worked for a local stage line and lived in the early Pilot Butte Inn. A bachelor, he spent a great deal of his time traveling, both for business and pleasure. While he was in the San Francisco area caring for his aging father, Davies purchased a piece of equipment that was destined to play a significant role in Claude's life — a 1908, two-cylinder Rambler motorcar.

After purchasing the Rambler,

Davies had it shipped from San Francisco to Portland via the steamer, "Beaver." When it arrived in Portland, the car was put on the river steamer, "Bailey Gatzert," and delivered to the dock in The Dalles on the Columbia River. He then drove it down from The Dalles to Bend via the stage and freighter's roads.

Gasoline was a scarce commodity in the early 1900's and was expensive — even by today's standards. Davies had to wait until he had enough money to buy fuel before he could bring his new autocar to Bend. And, after arrival, travel in the Bend area was governed by the supply of dollars for fuel.

In 1908, there were only two motorcars in Bend. One has survived and is on display in Bend's Pioneer Museum.

That same year — just before school was out — Davies took Claude and a group of his school chums out to Shevlin Park for their annual school picnic. In doing so, he gave many young people their first ride in a gasoline-powered motorcar. Needless to say, Claude photographed the event.

In the summer of 1909, the Alaska Yukon Pacific Exposition was in full swing 300 miles north of Bend — at Seattle. Davies had been to the Portland World's Fair four years earlier and was so caught up in the excitement that he hurried down to Bend to tell his family about the exciting events at the fair. The tales of the exposition caught the imagination of 16-year-old Claude, and his fondest

wish was that he might get to go. The more his uncle talked about the fair, the more the Kelley family felt it was something they just shouldn't pass up.

"But how will we get there?"

Davies had the answer.

"We'll drive the Rambler to the steamer docks at The Dalles," he said. "From there, we can go downriver on the 'Bailey Gatzert' to Vancouver and take the train to Seattle."

The prospects of such a trip boggled the mind of young Claude.

On to Seattle

A shout of exultation went up in the Kelley household when Davies and Claude's father announced that the family would go to the Seattle exposition. In talking about it today, Claude puts it this way:

"Well, we all had to go. We loaded the family into the Rambler. Mother carried my baby brother, Harold, in her arms. Father helped my uncle drive — and pushed. My brothers, Lloyd and Hugh, and my sister Susie, and me, of course, plus all the luggage made a pretty good carfull. Boy, what a sight it was!"

Luggage was strapped onto the running boards and over the hood as well as in the "trunk" in the rear. The right side of the hood was left clear so that the driver could see. (The steering wheel of the Rambler was on the right side.)

As Kelley recalls the trip, there were two basic problems — one was the so-called "road," and the other was the supply of gasoline. And, right

WALL Street near the corner of Oregon Avenue looking west. 1911.

om the start, the trip was an adven-
re. They had no sooner left the out-
irts of Bend before the first problem
ared itself — the "road."

In the summer of 1909, freight wag-
is and stages had churned the road-
ay into axle-deep dust and ruts that
l but swallowed the wheels of the
w-fangled gasoline buggy. The
gh center of the roadway offered no
oblem to the horses and wagons;
t, to the automobile, it was a king-
zed obstacle — just as it is today.
he Rambler, as Claude remembers
had a chain drive that went from a
anetary transmission to the open
ar end. As the Rambler went over
e road's high centers, the chain
ound into the dust and rocks. If the
r didn't hang up on the high center,
en the chain would. Time after
ne, the family would dismount,
sh and mount up again ... only to
ve to go through the same routine
thin a mile or so. At the end of the
st day's drive-and-push, they had
tten all the way to the base of Cow
nyon just north of Madras.

An excerpt from the dairy Claude
pt on the trip describes some of the
nily's problems on the first day:

"There were no other towns until
came to Madras at 1:45 (they had
t Bend at 8:10). We got 2 gallons of
soline from the Madras Trading
., the only gasoline they had.

"We went along fairly well until
0 when we punctured a tire. It took
minutes to change tires. We went
right for a few miles until we came
an uphill pull through deep dust
l a high center in the road. We

EQUIPMENT for the first powerplant in Bend is hauled into town by this 12-horse string pulling two wagons. 1910.

ALL GRADE school in Bend, 1908.

CLAUDE'S mother (left) and his cousin, Mary Caroline Davies, in 1910. Trout were from the Deschutes River near Bend. Large ones were Dolly Vardens and small ones rainbows.

STARTING for home after Bend High School's annual school picnic, 1911.

GOING deer hunting in September 1912. Left to right: John Bates, Claude's brother, Lloyd, Claude's father, and John Carmody, co-owner of Bend confectionery and pool hall.

could not pass the place without turning out of the road into the sagebrush which was about 4 feet high and 3 inches in diameter. This was a hard thing to do because the ground was soft and the road was cut down so far that the wheels would not go up. Finally, we backed down to where the road was better and hit off through the sagebrush. Some of us walked because we did not want to get stuck. By turning and dodging some of the biggest bushes we got to good road again."

There was really no need for anyone to write down the "rules of the road" in 1909. When a loaded freighter pulled by six to ten horses and carrying everything from corsets to sugar and salt and canned beans started down Cow Canyon from the railhead at Shaniko, it had the right-of-way.

All the freighters had a string of bells hanging on their lead team. The bells were the song of the long-line skinners as they traveled through the juniper and sagebrush country. It was the bells that warned freighters coming from the opposite direction. In Cow Canyon, meeting a freighter part way up was a nightmare.

The Second Day
Bright and early the second morning, the family was up, had breakfast and started up Cow Canyon. For the men, there was no sense getting on the Rambler. They had to push it almost all the way to the top, anyway. Time after time, the Rambler would fall into the ruts left by the steel-rimmed wheels of the freighters; and, time after time, it had to be pushed out. The sun was almost at its zenith when Antelope flat came into view. With a sigh of relief, the men climbed onto the Rambler and chugged along toward Shaniko.

Today's travelers have little or no problem finding gasoline. But, in 1909, things were a bit different. Although they did find two gallons of gasoline in Madras, their first "sure" place to get gasoline was at Shaniko (they hoped). There had been fuel available at Shaniko the year before when Claude's uncle drove down from The Dalles, but there was no guarantee it would be available this time.

When they rolled up to the store in Shaniko amid barking dogs and shouting children, they were relieved to see the stack of gasoline cans on the porch in front of the store.

"We've made it this far. We'll make 'er all the way, now."

After filling up with gasoline and taking a few minutes for resting, the travelers set off again for Bakeoven and Shearer's Bridge where they would cross the Deschutes River. The grade down to the bridge was almost a repeat of the Cow Canyon trip — only downhill. The ruts were almost as deep, and dust covered everything and everyone. Claude's father paid the $1.00 toll to cross the bridge, and they chugged across and headed up the grade toward Dufur.

Dufur was a welcome sight for the tired, dusty travelers. They pulled up in front of the Dufur Hotel to the stares of the local townspeople. After a bath and a night's rest, the Kelley's rolled on, arriving in The Dalles about noon of the next day. (Not too bad a trip, only two and half days from Bend to The Dalles.)

Down the Columbia

All along the trip, Claude had been taking photos of their adventure. As he stood on the dock listening to the blast of the "Bailey Gatzert's" steam whistle as it came into The Dalles to take the Kelley's to Vancouver, Claude knew that this trip would be something he would remember for many years to come — camera or no camera.

On the trip down the Columbia, Claude and his family took in the sights and sounds of a growing Oregon. This was before the days of barge traffic on the Columbia. Wheat was carried by rail. Steamboats carried only what they could put on board.

As they approached Vancouver, they saw the giant drawbridges that opened and closed to let river traffic through. From Vancouver, they took a trolley to Portland where they stayed with another uncle for a couple of days before boarding a train for Seattle.

The Seattle Exposition was one of many hundreds of events Claude Kelley was to photograph over the decades in the Pacific Northwest.

"I bought a new Eastman folding Kodak in Seattle," Claude remembers. "It was the latest thing. It took postcard-size photos. I wish I could remember how much it cost, but I don't."

As photographic techniques became more and more sophisticated, Claude kept updating his cameras and darkroom equipment. As Bend and Central Oregon grew, Claude was there to photograph the current events that make history.

Someday, without a doubt, there will be many historians and scholars who will thank Claude Kelley and his camera for recording the growth, progress and historical events that mark the evolution of the little wayside along the Deschutes known as Bend.

PARADE passes the corner of Wall Street and Oregon Avenue. 1916.

BUILDING the high bridge over the Crooked River. 1911. The north half was erected first then the material lowered to the bottom of the canyon and hoisted to the rim to build the south half.

WORKMEN had to go down this 320 foot rope ladder to reach their positions on the canyon floor.

Little Known Tales from Oregon History

An early-day license plate from Eddie Campbell's airplane.

No. 9
Pioneer Pilots of the

By Jim Anderson

The early days of aviation in Central Oregon were filled with forced landings and enough close calls to turn a modern pilot's hair white. Ted Barber was the first successful commercial aviation pioneer to operate a business in the area. His first plane was a WACO 9, powered by an OX-5 engine.

The WACO was the mainstay of the early aviation businesses throughout the country; and the OX-5 engine, a leftover from WW I, was the most easily aquired engine to power the early airplanes. Unlike commercial or general aviation today where power failures are as uncommon as once in 5000 engine operating hours, in the early 20's and into the 40's a power failure was all too common. A vital part of training for pilots was the eventual emergency landing without power.

To Ted Barber there were only a few times when such events were in reality an "Emergency." He had flown the OX-5 powered WACO for so long he knew just about when it was going to quit and was always prepared for it. It is a somewhat dubious honor for the OX-5. It was at least dependable in the pilot knowing it was going to stop at least once in ten flights — he could depend on it. Like the time he and Al Mansfield were going to fly from Bend to Eugene, a route that would take them over the McKenzie Lava Fields.

The year was 1931, Al was one of

Ted's students and was needing a cross country flight. They had talked the flight over; and finding the weather was good all the way, they took off from Knotts Field in clear blue sky. The old OX-5 purred like the preverbial kitten as the WACO, now completely rebuilt and painted a gleaming silver, climbed into the clear Central Oregon sky.

Al was at the controls as the airplane was slowly passing the snow-capped crags of North Sister. Ted was seated in the front seat and had been watching over the side at what Al thought was some scenic view below him. Ted turned himself around in the seat and unfastened his seat belt, then shouted to Al.

"We've got a water leak, Al! I'm going to go out on the wing and see where it's coming from!"

KNOTT FIELD 1929, otherwise known as the Bend Airport. Ted Barber is standing next to his combined office and home — a tent. The trusty WACO 9 is parked in the background.

Al started to say something else . . . but it was too late. Ted was already heaving his leg over the edge of the cockpit and swinging onto the lower wing. The OX-5 was a water cooled engine and a big radiator was mounted on the front of the WACO for cooling the engine fluid. Ted thought there might have been a rupture in the radiator plumbing. If that were so, it would be better to land somewhere near Indian Ford or Black Butte rather than on a smooth spot in the McKenzie lava fields — where such smooth places were difficult to find.

Al had a hard time watching Ted as he slowly inched forward through the rigging wires to a spot where he could see the water cooling plumbing and radiator connections. Peering into the cowling, he pushed here and there. Then after what Al thought was an unreasonable length of time for anyone to be standing on a wing 3,000 feet above the surface without parachute, Ted slowly inched his way back to the cockpit.

As he was again safely inside the airplane, he turned to Al and shouted, "She's okay Al. It's just the packing around the water pump! I think it'll last until we get to Eugene. Then he gave him that easy going Barber "smile" and turned around to enjoy the rest of the flight — smiling.

Ted Barber was one of those fortunate people who had the pleasure to learn about flying from one of the great pilots of all time, Oregon's own

PIONEERING TEAM. Ted Barber stands alongside his WACO 9 parked on Knott Field in Bend in 1929. He purchased the airplane for $1,600 on the day he received his license and went into the flying business that was to keep him flying for 40 years. Fuel line failures were responsible for numerous power-off landings in pastures and fields through Central Oregon. Yet, in his long career, Ted never had a passenger injured nor had a student who had an accident in an aircraft.

Photos Courtesy of Ted Barber

Sage Brush Country

...ex Rankin. Tex was a great aerobatic ...ilot of the late 30's and into the 40's. ...e could make an airplane do just ...bout anything he wanted it to do ... ...nd then some. It was Tex who gave ...ed the spirit of flying that has taken ...im through some exciting times, that ...o some people would amount to a ...erilous flight. Ted has a unique ...hilosophy about flying, stated this ...ay ...

"I was never one to back away from ...dventure in an airplane. I always ...gured airplanes were made to fly, ...nd I was made to fly them."

Looking back through Ted's 47 ...ears of flying, it is accurate to say ...hat he never has backed away from a ...ight and probably has never missed ...ving his life a little richer than many ...eople. Like the time he flew the ...ome built airplane that Bob and Earl ...tevens of Bend had built.

Finding the wood, fabric and iron ...o build a small airplane wasn't too ...uch trouble in the early days of the ...0's. A person with an average ...mount of aeronautical engineering ...r acquainted with airplanes fairly ...ell could (and often did) make a ...ome built airplane. But finding a ...mall, lightweight engine to power ...ne plane was always a problem. ...at's why in the early days of aviation, ...iders were easier to find and fly ...an airplanes. But in this case, the ...evens Brothers built a very clean, ...ght little parasol-type airplane and ...owered it with a Model "T" Ford

engine. On a clear, warm summer day the Stevens Brothers rolled their new airplane out to Knotts Field and, calling Ted, announced they had brought it out for him to fly. Ted walked around it and looked it over very carefully. He liked their workmanship and patted them both on the back.

It was late afternoon. The air had cooled down and had gotten a little "thicker" when Ted got the Ford engine going on Steven's airplane. He warmed it up and taxied to the very end of the field. Once against the fence, he turned the little home built around and, with the throttle wide open, lunged down the field. The plane rolled slowly at first. Then, as it picked up speed, the tail slowly raised off the ground. At about the half way point across the field, Ted eased back on the stick and the ship bounced into the air ... but quickly settled back to earth again. Again he pulled back on the stick, and again the ship flew to about ten feet above the ground ... and landed again. Time after time Ted would yank the little plane up; but, time after time, it would come back down. Disappointment showed on the Stevens' boys faces as Ted taxied the little home built back to their car.

"Let's wait until we get a little wind boys," he announced. "We'll give her a try again." Everyone agreed. Two days later, a perfect breeze was blowing across the sandy

BEND AIR SERVICE, 1933. The proud fleet of the Bend Air Service as it looked at Knott Field (site of the Knott Landfill today). The planes are the WACO 9 and 10. The WACO 9 is on the right. Note the "rabbit ear" top wingtips and exposed OX-5 engine. The WACO 10 had a smooth wing tip, and the OX-5 engine was enclosed.

"runway" of Knotts Field.

This time, Ted took the Ford-powered home built to a point diagonally across the field, this would give him the longest run possible. With a cloud of dust, the little plane went speeding across the sand ... faster ... faster ... and suddenly Ted pulled it into the air. The cheers were wild from the spectators and above them the Stevens Brothers were shouting, "Hey, look ... we told you so! It will fly ... it does fly!!" Ted and the tiny home built slowly climbed. But, at about 300 feet above the ground, the aircraft stopped climbing and began to slowly sink again. Cheers were suddenly stopped as the plane became a speck headed north across the lava fields and sage brush — slowly sinking from the sky.

Ted was pretty busy as he watched the boundry of the airport slide by beneath the descending home built. He dared not turn to the left or right for fear of stalling the little plane and crashing, so he kept on straight ahead. About two miles ahead of him there was a clear space in the sagebrush, but the lava fields were looking too rough for a landing that would save the airplane. His only hope was a big field about seven miles from his takeoff point. He wondered how long the little Ford engine could hold out, going full throttle.

He turned and looked to see how far he had come from the airport. What he saw made him turn a little chillier . . . a long cloud of steam was coming from beneath the aircraft where the radiator was mounted. He had about five miles to go and wondered if he would ever get there . . . but . . . as it was with many of Ted Barber's flights, he calculated the endurance of the mechanical device he staked his life on and won. Seven miles from the airport, the little home built was landed . . . at full throttle and steaming like a brass kettle. As the plane rolled to stop, several cars and loud cheers from delighted occupants greeted Ted. They had almost run the seven miles faster than the home built.

Many other attempts had been made in the area of home built aircraft. Tom Huettle and his brother built a good looking airplane; but, from all the stories collected, it never flew, even though Tom did his best to make it leave the ground at a small field located about where KGRL is today. The story is that Tom wouldn't give up even though he was headed for the barn — and apparently that's where he ended up — flying, or rather, driving the little home built right into the barn — through the barn doors!

Eddie Campbell of Prineville was another home builder of significant accomplishments. He got the bug for flying when he was in his teens going to high school in Prineville.

There is a story about Eddie building and attempting to fly a hang glider in those days. From reports, he apparently got the glider away from the cliff edge overlooking the city. Then, when the momentum was gone, the kite and Eddie crashed to the earth in a pile of wood splinters and light canvas — perhaps one of the earliest

CURTISS PUSHER. Powered by a three-cylinder Zeekley that put out about 35 hp, this 1934 plane was used by Ted Barber on many training flights. A cylinder head once flew off the Zeekley and hit Selby Towner of Bend smack on the head while they were in flight. The Pusher had a 39 ft. wingspan and flew so slowly that a man could almost run alongside it while in flight. One day, Ted Barber and Pat Gibson of Bend were chasing a coyote across the sagebrush. Pat reached out and grabbed the coyote by the tail, almost lifting it off the ground.

"Back to the drawing board" events in Central Oregon. But the real accomplishment of Eddie's flying career of home built airplanes took place in his "STORMS FLYING FLIVER."

Early in 1930, Eddie got the plans and the desire to build the "Flying Fliver." It took him several weeks to assemble all the materials — spruce, J.C. Penney's top grade of cottonsheeting — and to rebuild a Model "A" Ford automobile engine that would work in his fliver. At the time Eddie was working for the Ford Garage in Prineville and had access to all the materials he was going to need to modify the Ford engine. He had the help of his school teacher, Jack O'Keefe, and his school chum, Billy Jacobs, as he went to work on the fliver. This was the first such accomplishment for the then 23-year-old Eddie, and one that was going to live with him for the rest of his life.

At last, the time came when the brand new shiny aluminum-painted STORMS FLYING FLIVER was taken to the Prineville Airport. Eddie and Ted had everything pretty well arranged. Ted was, as usual, going to fly the new airplane first; then it would be Eddie's turn. That was the way it was planned — but it didn't work out that way.

To a man who dreams about flying his own airplane some day and having it right there on the field, the thought of someone else flying it first doesn't seem too fair . . . and that's the way it was with Eddie. Ted had been away now for four days on another flying job — and there sat the new bird.

"I'll do it," Eddie decided. He got Billy Jacobs to come out and be his "chase man." It was necessary for a

car to follow him down the runwa and signal him when he reache 35 mph — flying speed — as there w only one instrument in the airplane home-made tachometer that didn work very well.

Eddie started the engine and bega to make faster and faster runs up ar down the runway. Each trip he we faster and faster. At last, he reache the magic speed of 35 mph, and eased back on the stick. The litt plane stuck to the ground, not wan ing to fly.

He stopped at the end of the ru way, turned around and tried it agai This time, he was headed into t slight wind. When the signal came f the right speed, he eased back on t stick again, only this time a little fu ther. The airplane eased off t ground, flew a few yards and settle down again, apparently not wantir to fly.

Eddie shut the Ford down, and and Billy had a design discussio They both decided that the proble was that the aircraft was nose heav Eddie got to looking at his hand work; and, in his words, he "move the wing ahead a jog."

The next day, Billy and Ja O'Keefe went to the airport wi Eddie, and they started the engine the fliver again. This time, Edd didn't hesitate as he rushed down t runway. When the signal came f 35 mph, he hauled back on the stic and immediately the little plane sh into the sky. This time there was hesitation, the nose of the aircr kept rising, higher and higher. Edd pushed the stick further forward, b the nose wouldn't come down. In moment, the little plane had zoome

During one period of his flying career, Ted Barber flew supplies of all kinds to ranchers in the remote areas of Central and Eastern Oregon. Note the load of irrigation pipe tied onto the wing supports of his Cub.

to over 100 feet above the surface and was headed straight up . . . something had to give.

On the ground, both Jack and Billy were thrilled to watch the fliver leap into the sky and shoot upward. They watched as it climbed and cheered Eddie on. Suddenly their cheers caught in their throats as the little plane climbed steeper and steeper and then right before their eyes it came to a complete stop . . . standing on it's tail!

The little Model A Ford engine roared on in defiance of gravity, but to no avail. With a wink of an eye, the fliver suddenly swapped ends. The nose pitched over as it went into a full stall and then a sickening tail spin straight to the ground. The roaring engine suddenly stopped as the silver plane slammed into the ground going straight down! Both men couldn't believe their eyes.

"Eddie's killed!" Jack shouted. Silence settled over the sagebrush and juniper as the little plane sagged

Eddie's shoulders to get him out, fearful of a fire at any moment. But try as they might, Eddie was a part of his airplane in more ways than one.

"Hey, you guys! Take it easy, will you!" Eddie then explained the situation. "My feet are stuck right through the firewall. You've got to get a saw and cut me out." And that's what they did.

Several hours later, the two men carried Eddie into Dr. Adkisson's office where Eddie was checked over and released as a whole person. He had a cracked skull that the doctor knew of. But, for a Scotsman, that wasn't severe enough to put him into bed. A week later as a big yellow and purple mark began to show on his leg, Eddie discovered he also had a broken leg.

Experiences like these didn't stop Eddie Campbell from furthering his flying career. He went on and got his state license, then his federal license and flew a long list of airplanes from the old 35 hp Aeronca C-3 to an Eagle-

and women who received their pilot's certificates. Many of them, especially in the early days, were students of Ted Barber. Many flew in the old WACO 9 and, later on, in the newer WACO 10 that was the pride and joy of the Bend Flying Service.

Ted made many memorable flights in the WACOs, some of them more exciting than others. Many people in Bend remember the time that he had the same old gas line problem over Bend and landed the WACO on Newport Avenue. Everything would have gone along fine if he hadn't had a handicap of a string cross wind on the Newport "runway" and no brakes to keep on the straight and narrow of the road. With a sickening crunch, he heard both wings as the airplane veered into a powerpole and slid to a stop. Ted and his student jumped out and were standing in the crowd that had gathered listening to the conversation.

"Hey, do you think they've already taken away the pilot?"

"Was the pilot killed?"

"Yeah, must have been."

But the next day, the WACO was back in the airport having the wings repaired, and Ted was ready to fly again.

Perhaps one of the most exciting parts of Ted's life in airplanes was his days of herding horses by air. During the depression years when general aviation and many other businesses began to fade away, Ted decided he liked to fly and wanted to stay in the flying business. He took his plane, the old WACO 10, off into the desert to transport "anything for anybody that was legal." He carried fence posts, wire, salt blocks, cowboys and nails. But it was in the area of herding horses that he found his place as a pioneering pilot in the Oregon country.

WARM-UP TIME. In the winter, aircraft oil can become so thick in the engine that starting it is somewhere between difficult and impossible. This is a homemade engine heater built by Ted Barber to warm his engine on cold winter mornings when he and his crew were driving horses in southeastern Oregon and northern Nevada in the 1930's and 40's.

into a pile of splintered wood, J.C Penney's sheeting and silver dope. There was no sign of life in the debris. Jack couldn't move. It was Billy who suddenly pushed him into the car. "Come on Jack!" he yelled. "We've got to get him out of there!" The car lurched ahead, and they sped to the scene of the crash.

Both men started yanking on

rock biplane, on to a 40 hp Cub and, finally, his pride and joy, a 165 hp Stinson. With his wife, "Babe," Eddie Campbell has flown over almost all of the great land we call home here in the sage and juniper of Central Oregon.

In the more than 40 years that aviation has been growing in Central Oregon, there have been many men

It was already there, right in front of him, the rock strewn crown of the Mountain.

It was on a horse herding trip into Snow Storm Mountain country of Northern Nevada that Ted and his loyal WACO 10 parted company. It was in the fall of 1933 that Ted found himself chasing a big bunch of horses towards the wing corrals on the lower desert with the beat up can clanging along behind him. He had just made a low pass and bounced the kerosene can off the tail end of a big stallion that was trying to lead the group away and was pulling up into a steep climbing turn when the disease of the WACO fuel system struck. The powerful Comet Radial engine he had installed to replace the ancient OX-5 suddenly quit — dead. There was no time to pick a place to land. It was already there, right in front of him, the rock strewn crown of the Mountain. He slammed the stick forward to gather flying speed and with ability of a longtime pilot leveled off for what was bound to be one of the worst and roughest landings of his life — if not his last. The WACO's big wheels collided with the rocky ground, and immediately the plane bounced into the air and bounced again. He was landing in a stout tail wind, going downhill and beating the airplane to pieces.

"There's no way this airplane can hold together," he thought. For the first time in his flying over 2,000 hours, he elected to leave the plane before it stopped. He pulled the catch on the seat belt and somehow managed to keep the plane rightside up. At about 30 mph, he thought it was about to break up so he leaped over the side of the cockpit and came face first into the hard rocky surface of the mountain. He was knocked unconscious and rolled into a senseless heap. The airplane kept rolling through the rocks and suddenly flipped over on its back with a crunch as wings, tail and fuselage buckled. Silence settled over Snow Storm Mountain as man and airplane lay crippled — perhaps both fatally.

In about an hour, Ted came around and slowly looked at the mess he was in. His airplane was about 100 yards ahead of him, lying on its back. He was alive but conscious of a great deal of pain in his face. He felt the deep gashes around his mouth, the spaces where teeth had been. He could see the blood on the ground where he had landed after leaving the plane.

"Wish I had stayed with it," he reflected. Then, thinking about the cold, he stumbled to the airplane, found some matches and got a safe distance away from the gasoline to build himself a fire and wait for help. It was after he had the fire going that he almost did what the crash didn't do. After the fire was going good, made of scrub sage and grass, he passed out again and this time fell into the fire.

Ten miles away in the lower desert, his crew was beginning to feel uneasy about his not returning and set out to find him. Over three hours after he crashed, the horsemen spotted the WACO lying on its back and galloped over to assist Ted. The next few days were torture for Ted as his face began to be overhauled. But perhaps more painful than the bodily injury he suffered was the loss of his airplane — a tool that, to Ted Barber, was like his right hand.

For all the adventures that the early pioneer aviators lived through in their quest to make a living, there were hundreds of thousands of hours that were flown without incident. Mails were delivered, people were taken on barnstorming flights, all without incident. There were lives saved by pilots who brought news to anxious parents or medicine to victims of disease and accident.

The list of pioneer pilots of the Central Oregon country is a long one. This writer has only talked to a tiny segment of this group. In future editions, we hope to bring you more tales of flying in this area.

Ted Barber lives today in a sprawling valley of northern Nevada where he works with his wheel chair for sick livestock, his leaf cutter bees for polinating alafalfa seed, his soon-to-be-solar-heated greenhouse, his primary flight trainer, his wife, Margaret, and his memories of a life filled with the true adventure of living and doing what suits a man best.

Little Known Tales from Oregon History

Shorty Gustafson standing beside the 1912 Cadillac somewhere near Chemult.

Photos by Shorty Gustafson

No. 10
Driving Motor Stages in the Mid-1920's

By Dean Hollinshead

In the mid-1920's, the early motor stages which thundered up and down Central Oregon highways had all the fascination for the young men of the day that jet airliners and space travel have for the young men of the 1970's.

I know. I was hooked on 'em from the very first one I saw.

I got my first job driving a motor stage for Jess Hunsaker from Bend to Klamath Falls in May of 1924 and continued driving for George Duke's Central Auto Service until the spring of 1926 when I started my own line without even a shoestring to start with. But that didn't stop me. I didn't have enough money to buy a tire — much less enough to buy three cars which I needed to operate a stage line.

I figured it didn't do any harm to dream, so I went to LaPine where my brothers were operating the store and two solid-tired freight trucks. While I drove one of the trucks, I kept dreaming about my own stage line. I talked to my brothers about it, but they were just as broke as I was — and that was real broke.

Just about that time, I met a car salesman from The Dalles. He sold seven-passenger Big Six Studebakers which was just what I needed. He had one of 'em with him. He told me that I could make a small down payment on the Studebaker and let the car pay for itself. I managed to scrape together enough for the down payment — I've forgotten how much it was, but I do remember that I owed about $1,000 on it, and the monthly payments were $45.

Then I met Bob Elliot, a driver who was running from Bend to Eugene. When I told him about my idea, he

First run out of Bend from Frenchie's Stage Depot which was located on Bond Street between Oregon and Greenwood Streets. Man in white shirt facing camera is Bob Elliot.

said that he had a seven-passenger Hudson and would like to go in with me.

We had two cars but needed one more. We had heard about a seven-passenger Cadillac at the Bend Garage. It was a privately-owned car and was in good shape. We figured it was just what we needed to round out our "fleet" of motor stages. I don't think Cecil and I had a dime between us when we went into the Bend Garage to see Walter Combs.

We told him about our plans, and he listened. He really seemed interested. Then I hit him with what I was afraid would end the conversation.

"But we don't have any money."

Walter leaned back in his chair and smiled before answering.

"There's always ways to get around that if you're serious about your plans and know what you're doing," he said. "I know you boys, and I think we can work something out.

"I'll tell you what. I'll sell you the

Cadillac for $500. I'll take your contract on the Studebaker for the $250 down payment on the Cad. You can pay me off for $50 a month. How's that?"

We thought it was great.

Actually, I had enough money in the bank to make two payments on the Cadillac and to keep the cars rolling for about two months. But you know? I never did have to use any of that money in the bank. The cars paid for themselves right from the start.

My brother, Cecil, and I went down to Salem and filed with the P.U.C. to operate a passenger stage line between Bend and Klamath Falls and wildcat into Odell Lake and down the Natron Cutoff into Chemult. With three, seven-passenger cars, we were ready to go into business. Our final detail was making arrangements to operate out of French's Stage Depot in Bend. We were launched on our big adverture.

The following Monday morning at

Eleven-passenger 1924 Studebaker bus which the author leased occasionally for the run between Weed and Dunsmier, California.

Filling station at Weed, California, where buses were serviced. Shorty Gustafson at left and Dean Hollinshead at right.

8:30, we pulled all three cars up at the Depot and found 22 passengers waiting for us.

I darned near dropped dead. But, as luck would have it, I survived.

One car went straight through to Klamath Falls. One went to Chemult, then north up the railroad right-of-way as far as the Tylor Construction Camp and back into Bend. I took the Studebaker and went to Odell Lake and south down the right-of-way as far as Chemult and back to Bend. We had to hire one driver, Leo Ordway, to drive the Cadillac until Cecil could get on the job.

All the roads were dirt, and rough and dusty. Our top speed was about 30 to 35 miles an hour, so it took all day to make these trips.

That first year, we had lots of passengers. Then the construction gangs began to finish off their jobs and move out. But even at that we seemed to get our share of passengers. Our competitor was my old employer, Central Auto Service.

We kept the Hudson driven by Bob Elliot and the Cadillac driven by Cecil on through run from Bend to Klamath Falls. If they had any passengers for any of the construction camps and I wasn't around, they'd have to detour around by the camps.

Believe me, running a bus line in those days wasn't like it is now. We didn't show up at the depot and find a load of passengers waiting for us.

No sir. You had to go out and find your own passengers. Like meeting the train from Portland which arrived in Bend at 7:00 in the morning. It was up to you to talk them into riding on your stage. Almost every morning, there'd be several men going to Chemult and up the railroad right-of-way as far north as Odell Lake. It was up to each driver to meet the train and get his fair share of passengers — or more than his share if he could get away with it.

Most of these men came out of Portland on a pass from the company employment office. Their bus fare was then held out of their wages after they had worked long enough.

These passes were usually marked as to which stage line they were supposed to take from Bend, but some of the men preferred to pay their own way. They were the ones the drivers were looking for, because they were fair game. When we met the train, we picked up all we could haul and took them up to our office where the Bend employment man would tell them which car to take.

Most all of the men with money went with us, because we saved them a long walk from the railroad station uptown. The others would remember us when they quit and came back into Bend. The only disadvantage we had was that our bus had to leave our office 30 minutes later than our competition, because that's the way our P.U.C. permit was set up.

We got along real good with most of the men in charge of each construction office by doing them a few favors from time to time. Lots of times when ordering more men out of Portland, they would specify our line.

Our biggest block was Stewart & Welch at Odell Lake who had lots of men coming in. They sent men across Odell Lake by boat to camps which couldn't be reached by car. Central Auto Service got most of that trade except for the cash fares. But, thank the Lord, there were lots of them.

When it came time for the men to come out, we had to be right on the job to get our share, because Stewart & Welch had a deal where we couldn't get across the lake to talk to the men. So the competition between us and Central Auto Service got pretty exciting at times.

Quite often, I would stay around Odell Lake all day with very little to do. Some times, I would load up the car with young people and take them to Crescent Lake to go swimming. it was a big day for all those we could pack into the car.

Mr. White, the manager of the Stewart & Welch office, was no friend of mine; but he had a daughter about 17 years old who seemed to be kind of left out by the rest of the young set. They figured she might not like their crowd.

One day, I had the car loaded with young people on our way to Crescent Lake. When we went past her house, she was standing out in the yard. She looked so lonely and left out that I stopped.

"Hi," I said. "We're on our way to Crescent Lake to go swimming. Wanna go with us?"

"Sure," she said. "Just a minute."

She went into the house and was back right away carrying her bathing suit. From that time on, she was one of the bunch. I got to know her lots better.

"Why don't you ever haul passengers for my daddy?" she asked one day.

"Well, we just don't seem to get along too well," I said. "I don't know just why, but . . ."

"Then I'll have to change all that," she said.

Things went along the same way for a day or so and nothing happened. Then, one day, I had a little time to kill, because it was too early to start back to Bend. I left the one passenger I had in the car and walked down to the Lake. But, when I came back to the car, it was full of men and baggage. It was no time for asking questions, so I just got in and headed for Bend. As I drove past the girl's house, she was standing on the porch. She waved to me just as if to say, "I told you so."

From that time on, Mr. White would even let me come into his office if he had something or someone to send out on the stage.

ABOVE: The 1924 Studebaker Motor Stage. RIGHT: The Bend-Klamath Falls Motor Stage. BELOW: 1924 Studebaker "Big 6" at the summit of the old McKenzie Pass Road. Sitting in the motor stage is Lily Hoard, later Mrs. Dean Hollinshead.
(Photos courtesy of Mrs. Edith Masten Hollinshead.)

Every payday, we would pick up paychecks at the camps, get them cashed in Weed and take the money back. We had a very simple method of charging for this service. We simply kept the odd cents. For example, if the check was for, say, $56.95, we kept the 95¢ and returned $56.00. That was fine for the larger checks; but, if it were for a smaller amount — say, $10.95 — the customer wasn't quite as happy. You would be surprised at how much money we made in this way. It more than paid for our board.

A little candy store in Weed was operating a kind of "skin game" which Shorty and I turned to good use. The idea was that you drew numbers for cash prizes. We played it almost every night and were pretty lucky. We set up an account under the name, Shorty & Co., and let our winnings build up. When we needed anything, we simply charged it against the "company" account. When we left, we still had about $50 in credit coming; so we took it in cash. Some fun!

Every Saturday night, we would make about three round trips between the camps and Weed hauling the construction workers in to the "city" so they could have a little fun. Every time we picked up a worker, we charged him a round trip fare; because we knew he would be broke on the return trip. Beginning about 8:30, one car would leave Weed for camp about every hour until midnight. Then Shorty and I would pile into bed.

We even found that the design of the Studebakers was good for pocket money.

You see, the front of the back seat was much higher than the back. This meant that people sitting in the back had their knees higher than their

Bob Elliot (left) and the author on a snowy day near Chemult. Car is 1924 Hudson.

"rear ends." This meant that loose change — and, quite often, folding money — slipped out of their pockets and trickled under the rear seat. So, every Sunday morning, Shorty and I would make a run to each car where we lifted up the back cushions to pick up the loose money. And usually there was some little bit of it — thanks to the Studebaker design. Then we had a first-class brainstorm. We took a 2x4 and set it up edgewise under the front of the back seat. This not only made the car ride easier; but, more important, it increased our "take" from pocket money.

By the end of winter, work was slowing down, and it was hard to get workers to go out to camp from Weed. Some of the contractors wanted us to haul workers direct from Sacramento to camp.

I made the first round trip to Sacramento. Shorty would make two round trips from Weed to Grass Lake before starting for Sacramento. I would get back to Weed early in the afternoon and deliver my men up to whatever camp they were to go to and then go to bed. The next morning, I would get up and make two round trips to Grass Lake before heading for Sacramento, leaving as Shorty was coming into Weed from Sacramento.

This lasted during the month of June, but we helped to keep men on

the jobs. Sometimes, we would get a load from camp all the way through to Sacramento; but, since this was kind of stepping on the toes of the other stage businesses, we didn't do that too often. But it was a hard way to make a buck. One day, we would have a 20-hour day; but we'd get some sleep the next night.

By this time, the job was finished. We were out of work and ready to go home.

I made pretty good money in California, and Shorty and I had a lot of fun. I think I paid Shorty a check for about $700. He took one Studebaker and went to Oakland, California, to visit his mother and brother. I took the other car and came back to Bend.

I was sitting on top of the world. I had my bills paid. I owned two seven-passenger Studebakers and had about $3,000 in the bank. I felt real happy about that.

We lost out on the Bend-Klamath Falls run, because Northland Transportation came in here from back East with three big buses. That stopped us with our seven-passenger cars — but quick!

My next endeavor was a mail contract between Lakeview and Bend — but it kept me in those big old Studebakers I so dearly loved.

As the saying goes, I wouldn't go through the kind of driving we did again for a million dollars. But, at the same time, I wouldn't take a million dollars for the experiences that we had.

Looking at it realistically, I know that the cars they build in Detroit today are far superior to those seven-passenger Studebakers. But none of 'em have the romance, the feeling of adventure that you got from the old-timers.

I can leave Bend today and drive to LaPine in just about a half hour and still stay under the 55 mile speed limit. But I can remember taking all day to get from Bend to LaPine. That is, if the road was good.

On bad days, it took a little longer. But do you think I would trade between a 1925 Studebaker and a 1978 model car? Not on your life!

Dean's brother, Cecil, standing beside a truckload of wool. Each bag weighed 375 pounds.

Little Known Tales from Oregon History

Carrying the Mail Between Bend and Lakeview

No. 11

By Dean Hollinshead

They say that time and tide waits for no man; and, when you're running a stage line and you run out of customers, you're out of business. That's what Shorty Gustafson and I discovered in 1924-25 when the Southern Pacific Railroad finished the Natron Cut-Off between Oak Ridge, Oregon, and Weed, California.

Shorty and I were operating the Bend-Klamath Falls Stage Line and were hauling workers from Bend and Klamath Falls out to the work sites. But, believe me, when the railroad was finished, so was the Bend-Klamath Falls Stage Line.

First run to bite the dust was the Bend-Chemult-Odell Lake run. That took out three cars. The next casualty was the Bend-Klamath Falls run. Long about that time, the Northland Transportation & Stage Company came into Bend from some place back East with three big thirty passenger buses. That finished off our stage line in nothin' flat.

The reason was simple. No passengers, no money coming in.

Shorty and I did manage to keep two cars working out of Weed until the railroad was finished down there. But, when the railroad was finished, that *finished* us, too, leaving me with

not much of anything but three Studebaker Big Sixes and one Cadillac. And they don't make too good eatin'.

Actually, Shorty and I had managed to save a little money in Weed, so we weren't hurtin' too bad. Shorty went south to Orland, California, to visit his folks for a few days. I headed back to Bend by way of Portland.

When I got back to Bend, there wasn't much to do; and that suited me pretty well. Shorty came back north but only got as far as Klamath Falls where he stopped off and drove taxis for a year or so before returning to Bend.

A friend of mine, Earl Hackney, had just got a mail contract between Bend and Silver Lake. I heard he was looking for a driver, so I looked him up to ask for a job.

"How about me driving for you?" I asked Earl.

"All right," Earl said. "We'll pay you $125 a month and pay for your room when you stay overnight at Silver Lake."

So I was back driving again.

Earl and I met every day at LaPine and had lunch together before going on our merry way. That is, we usually did it that way. Only this day, it turned out different.

I hadn't known it, but it seems like the job I took had belonged to a man who had about six kids and a wife to support. But the first I knowed about it was when we met that day in LaPine.

"Well, Dean, you just bought a half interest in a mail contract as of this morning about 8:00," Earl said.

"How come?"

"When I got in to Silver Lake last night, everyone in town jumped on me for canning Mr. Reeder. All I could think of to say was that I'd sold you half interest in the contract," Earl explained. "You think it over for a few days. I'll sure sell you half if

Hauling wood for the hotel in Silver Lake through almost a foot of snow.

Dean Hollinshead Photos

you're interested."

I looked up my brother, Cecil, and talked it over with him. At that time, Cecil was driving for Bend-Portland Fast Freight.

"It looks pretty good to me," Cecil said.

Within a couple of days, Earl and I met again in LaPine. While we were having a cup of coffee, Earl wrote out

getting some money coming in," I reasoned. "It looks like all I've done up to now is spend money. At this rate, it won't be long before the well runs dry if we keep taking out and not putting anything back in."

But everything was going fine for Cecil and me. Cecil drove his own car and paid his own expenses. I did the same thing. Around the first of each

contract. By that time, we had logging trucks and the one through freight truck as far south as Lakeview.

As time went by, the mail contract we had bought expired in 1928; so I had to bid on it on my own this time. The new contract ran between Bend and Paisley for another four years. I submitted the low bid, so we were

Two of the Big Six Studebakers (above) used on Silver Lake run with Shorty Gustafson on the left and Dean's brother, Cecil, on right.

Dean Hollinshead standing beside truckload of hay (left) being hauled from Summer Lake to Silver Lake.

Come rain, snow or shine, the mail must go through — in this case, through several inches of snow in LaPine. Cecil Hollinshead is standing beside one of the Studebakers.

a contract; and I gave him a check for $3,000, making me a partner in a three-year mail contract and one five-passenger Studebaker Big Six. Earl and I stayed together about a year and a half. Then he sold his half to my brother, Cecil. That meant that the two Hollinshead brothers had a U.S. Mail contract. We stayed with it until 1932 when another man underbid us, so we lost it.

It was just about the time when Cecil bought out Earl Hackney that I started doing some serious thinking.

"Maybe it's about time to settle down, do some real work and start

month, we'd get together and split up the income before we were off again.

We had pretty good jobs, and we had lots of time for ourselves. The only hitch was that there was only so much money coming in with no way to increase it. We figured we ought to do something about that, so we bought out A. Gebhard Freight Line between Bend and Silver Lake.

That took another $3,000, and we needed an extra man for the truck. We hired Shorty Gustafson to drive the truck or stage — whichever was needed. Shorty stayed with us up until 1937 — long after we lost the mail

set up for another four years.

We hauled passengers, mail and express in the mail cars and all the heavy freight on the truck.

Shorty and I used to say, "We can haul anything that's loose at both ends and as far as the road is cut out." We did just about that, too. We had some wild trips with the freight truck. On most of the off-the-road trips, Shorty and I went together and came back together most of the time. There were two or three young fellows around who were always ready and willing to drive the mail stage for me when I went with Shorty on the freight truck. Two of the fellows I remember were Curtis Donahue and Arthur Harper.

One day, Shorty, Curtis and I got together at Silver Lake. Shorty was driving the truck and I had the mail car. Shorty had to make a run to Sand Springs which was way out on the desert. I decided I'd better go with Shorty, so I asked Curtis to take the mail on into Paisley for me.

Curt got down the road about eight miles out of Silver Lake. He failed to make one of the many turns in the road, so he cut across and turned the mail car upside down.

You think that bothered Curt any? Not a bit!

Curt knew a farmer, Everett Emory, in the area. Curt went to his house, borrowed Everett's car and headed for Paisley. While Curt was gone, Emory brought his team out to the car, rolled it over and towed it up to his farm house. By the time Curt got back from Paisley, the car was ready for him to try again.

Shorty and I got back from Sand Springs late that night. Early the following morning, I took the mail car and went to Bend. It was a week before I found out about Curt's accident.

But that's the way it was in those days. People helped people. And they never told stories on the other person.

For the most part, the mail stage run was pretty routine. It was something you did seven days a week, Sundays and all.

That is, it was routine except in the fall of the year when all the pretty young school teachers started arriving for the school year. Then it was far from routine.

There was only one stage line, so it was a sure thing that all of them would come in on our stage. That meant we had to wash behind our ears a little better each morning, be sure our neckties were on straight and be sure to meet the train in Bend. We weren't about to let those pretty girls walk all the way from the depot up to the stage office. No, sir!

We were never sure what day the new teachers would come in, but you could bet your bottom dollar that the Silver Lake Stage would meet every train until we were certain that all teachers had arrived. Sometimes, I wonder if those teachers knew how much special treatment they got.

We had no snow plows in those days. When it snowed, it just piled up on the road until it melted. You just put on your chains and worked your way through regardless of the snow's depth.

The first three years of our contract, we had three four-horse teams and an angle plow to help if we needed it. I think we only had to use the horses about a dozen times in the three years.

We put those Studebakers through snow that was so deep you'd have to stop and shovel the snow off the hood between the radiator and the windshield. It would get so deep on the hood that you could not see out of the windshield.

We kept one four-horse team at the Vandevert place near the present site of Sunriver, one at Summit Stage Station and one at Sam Almstead's Ranch near Freemont. Sam used to plow all the way from the stage station to Silver Lake and back. It took him three days to do the job.

Boy, was that living it up standing out there on that plow for about 10 to 14 hours at a time. Sam had lots of horses, so he used eight head on that long haul.

We used 35 x 5 high pressure tires on our cars. This put us up in the air about three inches higher than most cars, so all the people at Silver Lake would wait until the mail stage went through to Bend. They'd then try to follow us, but they usually got stuck on high centers. We could go right on around and would stop and pull them out. That would be the last we'd see of them, because they'd turn around and go back to Silver Lake, wondering how we could get through the snow when they couldn't.

We helped lots of people by pulling them out of mudholes or giving them a ride from one ranch to another. But, anytime we hauled anything or anybody, we charged for it. People knew why we had to do it, and no one ever kicked about our charges. It was just a part of the mail contract.

About this time, my four-year mail contract for the Bend-Paisley run expired. However, I decided to bid on the Bend-Lakeview contract and got it, giving me an additional four years.

We already had one car operating from Bend to Paisley; so, when I got the new contract, all I had to do was simply continue on to Lakeview with the same car. The mail run was just about the same, day after day. On the other hand, our anywhere-for-hire truck was different. We never knew where we were going or when we'd be back.

I took one job hauling 500 tons of loose rye hay from Thompson Valley Reservoir to Silver Lake for Jack O'Keefe. We were about two months getting this job completed, because we didn't haul every day. When we did haul, we made two trips a day with about seven tons on each load.

Shorty and I hauled 12,000 head of lambs from Silver Lake Marsh to Bly. While we were hauling these lambs, we never left the truck for 72 hours.

Shorty and I also hauled a few loads of hay from Summer Lake to Silver Lake. It didn't turn out to be a very good job, so we didn't haul much hay.

One day, we got unloaded at Silver Lake and started back for another load with Shorty driving. It was real cold. It was late in the afternoon when, all of a sudden, Shorty let out a big cuss word or two.

"My feet are so damn hot I can't stand it much longer," he said. I look down at Shorty's feet.

"Don't look now," I said, "but the truck's on fire."

Sure enough, it was. The hay and chaff had gotten down on the exhaust pipe and started a nice foot-warming fire which was burning right up through the floorboards right on Shorty's little pink tootsies. Believe me, Shorty got a hot foot — *but quick.*

No wonder he was complainin'.

Our most interesting hauls with our big truck was during wool shearing time which lasted about 45 days. We'd go from Silver Lake out to any shearing crew, pick up the wool and haul it to either Bend or Lakeview.

This job took two drivers on the truck all the time. I usually picked up the load at the shearing camp and hauled it back to Silver Lake. Then the other driver would take it on to Bend or Lakeview and come back to Silver Lake. He then went to bed, and I had to get up and go out after another load, regardless of the time. We never let the truck cool off from one trip to the next.

We hauled 42 sacks of wool on each load, and each sack weighed about 375 pounds. We had to load and unload by hand. So, by the time you'd made one of those runs, nobody had to tell you that you'd earned a rest.

The roads in them days weren't what they are now. They were crooked as a snake's back. The loads were always top-heavy, so we turned upside down more times than we could count. On just one day, my brother, Cecil, and I turned over three times between Cyaan Marsh and Silver Lake. On other days, we'd manage to stay rightside up all day.

I always looked forward to wool-hauling time. There were always so many bands of sheep around the shearing corral. I think they figured it took about 1,200 head to make up a band with only one man handling them. Sometimes, there would be four or five bands of sheep around the shearing corral at one time. My favorite passtime was watching the little lambs running and playing every night just before dark and again early in the morning.

We lost our mail contract to Lakeview in 1932, so I sold out my passenger and express business to the new bidder. I kept my freight truck and operated it until 1939 when I sold out to the Bend-Portland Truck Lines.

I've got a lot of years invested in those early days of automobiles and trucks. Between the passenger express and the mail contracts, I was on the run from 1920 to 1932; and, like I said, I stayed with the trucks until 1939. It was a good life. It was lots of fun. And it was never boring.

Not even for one minute, because you never know what was going to confront you around the next turn.

You can have your 1978 models. Personally, I'll stick to those big old Studebakers.

They was a man's car — every inch of 'em.

Little Known Tales from Oregon History

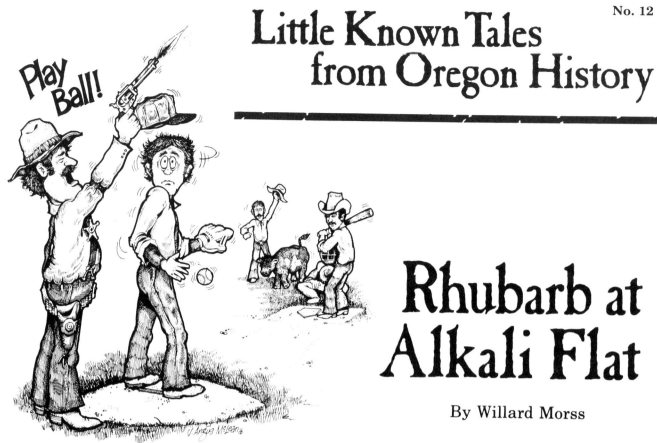

Play Ball!

Rhubarb at Alkali Flat

By Willard Morss

When the umpire showed up at the baseball game wearing a .45 pistol strapped on his hip, I guess I should've anticipated trouble. Of course, I was just a skinny 17-year-old at the time, and my only claim to fame was the ability to throw a sweeping, round-house curve ball.

At the designated time, the umpire walked out onto the pitcher's mound. He pulled out his .45 and fired a single shot into the air.

"I'm the umpire of this here baseball game," he announced. "If anyone wants to question my decisions, do so right now before the game starts."

He waved the .45 around for emphasis. The crowd loved it and gave him a cheer. He gave a mock bow and then threw back his head for the official announcement everyone had been waiting to hear.

"Play ball!"

It was the summer of 1915.

San Francisco was making a lot of noise about its Panama Pacific Exposition. Europe was in the second year of World War I. But neither of these events received more than passing attention from the residents of the small community of Roberts, Oregon.

Now, it won't do you any good to look for Roberts on today's Oregon map. It's not there. But, just for the record, Roberts was located on Alkali

Flat which is just south of the present location of Prineville Reservoir.

Anyway, the big news on Alkali Flat was the plans to expand the area's annual Fourth of July shindig to three days. There was to be a baseball game on July 3, a rodeo on the 4th and horse races on the 5th. There was to be an all-night dance on each of the three nights. So you can see that they were going all-out to provide a good time for everyone.

Alkali Flat had put together a team of local fellows who had a pretty good reputation for country baseball. About the only one I remember by name was the pitcher. His name was Marquard. He had a brother, Rube, who was a star pitcher for the New York Giants. Just three years earlier, Rube had stood the baseball world on its ear by winning 20 consecutive games for the National League team. Then, earlier in the 1915 season, Rube Marquard had pitched a no-hitter against the Brooklyn Dodgers.

I lived on Newsome Creek near Henry's Mill which was on the north end of the Maury Mountains. Since my sister was queen of the cook house at Henry's Mill, it was only natural that I would pitch for the mill team which was to travel to Alkali Flat on July 3.

Charlie Henry, who had moved onto Newsome Creek from the Paulina

country and built the sawmill some years earlier, was sending two wagonloads of people and ample picnic food to Alkali Flat for the game. Some of the mill folks planned to return home that night, but others were going to stay over for the following day's rodeo. Most of the ball players rode horseback so we could take a short-cut to Alkali Flat.

When we got to Alkali Flat, we were met by a fellow who was called "Old" Nelson. His nickname had nothing to do with his age any more than the title, "Kentucky Colonel," has to do with the military. It was sort of a badge of respect. He ran the Alkali Flat store. He was the un-official town mayor and was a genuine deputy sheriff. I guess that's why I didn't pay too much attention when Old Nelson kept his .45 pistol on his hip when he started umpiring the game.

From some of the stories around Alkali Flat, Old Nelson had quite a sense of humor. Seems that Alkali Flat had no jail, but Nelson had a big cellar under the store which worked just as well even though there was no light nor ventilation.

The story goes that, one night when Nelson was putting a loud, unruly prisoner into the dark, dungeon-like cellar, he called down to him as he was fastening the big padlock on the trap door:

"There's a big rattlesnake down there, so you'd better be careful."

After two hours in the dark with the imaginary rattlesnake, this fellow was a model of deportment at the all-night dances from that time on.

By noon, the two wagons from the mill had arrived. The women were laying out a huge picnic spread on a big table under the trees. The place was swarming with people. The celebration was getting under way. Wagons were parked under the big junipers. A stand was dispensing soft drinks. And, if you were interested in something harder, that wasn't too hard to find, either.

A few of those newfangled automobiles had shown up, too, belching out streams of fire and smoke. Seems like everyone was impressed with them except the horses. There was many a cussword said that day as ranchers tried to control their teams as the cars went by.

Lunch time was gossip time. Old friendships were renewed. News of weddings, births and deaths was passed back and forth. Everybody was in a holiday mood.

As game time approached, the crowd began to drift toward the diamond which was laid out in a nearby, freshly cut field. Benches had been set up for the spectators.

Being the out-of-town team, Henry's Mill went to bat first. And it didn't take us long to find out that throwing a baseball seemed to run in the Marquard family. He made mighty short work out of our hitters. Three up and three down.

Then I went out on the mound to face the Alkali Flat hitters, and I'll have to admit that I was pretty nervous.

"Just take it easy, young feller," Old Nelson urged me from his vantage point behind the mound. "They put their pants on one leg at a time."

I settled down enough to get the first two men out, but the third Alkali Flat hitter sent a long fly ball over the left fielder's head and made it all the way to third for a triple. I guess I was starting to get nervous again, because Old Nelson again urged me to take it easy. The next batter up hit a pop fly, and the inning was over.

From there on, the playing ran all the way from excellent to ridiculous. But, for the most part, it was the Alkali Flat team that was excellent and the Henry's Mill team ridiculous. By the end of the seventh inning, the score was 8 to 1 in favor of Alkali Flat. To put it bluntly, we were getting the pants beat off us.

Just as the eighth inning was about to begin, a small truck drove up and parked. Two cowpunchers got out of the truck and started walking toward the baseball diamond.

"Hey," someone yelled. "It's Johnny Muir and Billy Wray."

Practically all the male spectators abandoned the baseball game and rushed over to greet the newcomers.

The reason for all the excitement was Johnny Muir. Johnny was one of the top bronc riders from the Pendleton area. The Alkali Flat townspeople had taken up a collection and had raised $25 to pay him to ride broncs in the rodeo on the following day, but he had arrived a day early and had brought Billy Wray, another well known Pendleton bronc rider, with him.

Old Nelson held up the game and walked over to shake hands with Johnny and Billy and, as the unofficial mayor, to welcome them to Alkali Flat.

"Let's stop the game and start the rodeo," one of the buckaroos called to Old Nelson. He ignored the suggestion. Then other cowpokes took up the arguement. With Johnny Muir there to ride wild broncs, they had lost interest in the baseball game. But Old Nelson stood his ground. He insisted that the game was going the full nine innings.

Suddenly, there were wild yells from the direction of the temporary corrals which had been set up by one of the nearby ranches. Three buckaroos on horseback had opened the corral gate and were hazing the bunch of wild broncs toward the baseball diamond.

Spectators and ball players, alike, had to scramble to get out of the way to avoid being run down by the wild horses.

When the dust had cleared, it could be seen that one of the wild horses had been roped and thrown near second base. That bunch of rodeo-hungry cowpokes never gave that horse a chance. They descended on him like ants at a picnic. When the horse regained his feet, there was a rope around his neck and a half hitch on his nose. Within seconds, a saddle was cinched on him; and a buckaroo was in the saddle.

Ready or not, the rodeo was beginning a day early.

The bronc did its best to unseat the rider. It whirled and bucked as hard as it could for some ten to fifteen seconds. It then stood there trembling with the rider still in the saddle. A little urging got the horse to bucking again, but the rider had no difficulty in keeping his seat. The horse gave up.

The rider got a lot of cheers from the crowd. By now, the baseball game was completely forgotten.

The first horse was turned loose, and a second one was quickly saddled. Number two seemed too scared to buck and quickly gave up. He was

replaced by number three. This one did a little better, but the crowd was demanding more action. When numbers four and five disappointed the crowd, Old Nelson decided it was time for him to act. He could see that liquor was rapidly becoming a factor in the events — both among the buckaroos and the spectators.

He called Johnny Muir and Billy Wray over for a discussion on how to please the action-hungry crowd. While they were talking, a rancher from the Powell Butte country approached Nelson.

"My wife has a buggy horse that can out-buck that whole bunch of fuzztails," he said.

Old Nelson knew the horse, so he stepped up on one of the benches that had been vacated when the bunch of wild horses overran the baseball diamond and fired a shot into the air to get everyone's attention.

"We've finally located a bucking horse," Nelson told the crowd. "Our friend from Powell Butte has one which he says can out-buck any horse here. Do you want to see him ridden?"

"Yeah! Bring 'im on!"

A rider was sent to fetch the animal. He was a big, strong horse. Johnny Muir walked over to look at him.

"Mighty fine looking horse," he said.

I think every buckaroo there wanted to get the first shot at the Powell Butte horse. But, just at that moment, the rancher's wife — the owner of the horse — came over to see what was going on.

"What are you doing with my horse?" she said. She grabbed the horse's reins and started to lead it away. Her husband tried to reason with her, but he had had a little too much to drink to get her to change her mind.

When the crowd saw that she was serious about taking the horse back, they began to get ugly. They crowded around her, shouting and shoving.

Old Nelson and Johnny Muir quickly recognized her plight and came to her rescue. While Nelson quieted the crowd, Johnny led her and the horse away from the clamoring mob. He stroked the horse's neck, petted it, and openly admired the sleek animal.

"That's a mighty beautiful horse," he said. "I'd like to buy it from you."

"It's not for sale."

"Well, if you ever change your mind, you know where to find me."

By now, it was obvious that Johnny's attitude toward the horse was softening her attitude somewhat. Several of her friends who'd had less to drink than her husband urged her to let her horse be ridden.

"I'll let Mr. Muir ride the horse," she said. "But no one else."

Johnny thanked her and explained, "That will have to be up to Mr. Nelson."

Old Nelson scratched his head thoughtfully before answering.

"Well, that creates something of a problem," Nelson said. "You see, Mr. Muir is a professional rider. We invited him to Alkali Flat with the promise of paying him twenty-five dollars for his ride tomorrow, but there isn't enough to pay him for today."

This created another problem.

The local cowpunchers resented the payment to Johnny. They had to ride for free, and they couldn't see why Johnny Muir rated a special payment. Johnny simply ignored their comments and walked over to where Billy Wray was standing.

The local cowpokes then started appealing to the horse's owner, offering to ride it for free.

"Who needs Johnny Muir, anyway?" one called. "We're just as good as he is."

After a little more clamoring, the horse's owner hesitated and then spoke.

"All right," she said. "You can ride him under one condition. There will be absolutely no spurs."

She'd hardly gotten the words out of her mouth before a saddle appeared and was cinched on. Old Nelson then took charge, urging the crowd to move back and give the horse and rider room. He took a hat and put five numbered slips of paper in it. He handed the horse's owner the hat, and she held it while five eager riders drew slips to see in what order they would ride. A shout went up from the crowd when one of the cowpokes triumphantly held up the number one slip. They were ready for some real action now.

"Quiet! Quiet!" Old Nelson called. He waited until the crowd settled a little before continuing. "All rides will be by rodeo rules. If a bronc rider stays on for ten seconds, I'll fire a shot signalling the end of the ride. One of the mounted pick-up men will lift the rider from the saddle, and the next will have his turn."

That seemed agreeable with everyone.

The first rider mounted and, at a signal from Old Nelson, the horse was turned loose.

The big fellow whirled sharply about and gave two long jumps straight ahead and stopped dead in his tracks. The only trouble was — the rider kept on going and landed face first ahead of the horse.

"Two and one-half seconds," Old Nelson announced.

A mighty yell went up from the crowd and bottles were passing freely among the spectators and riders, alike.

The second rider lasted only two seconds, and the crowd went wild. Old Nelson stole a look at Johnny Muir, and they understood each other. They both knew they had to keep the show going.

The number three rider was the same cowpoke who had ridden the first horse and had ridden well. The crowd was hoping he would do as well on this one. When the horse was released, it made a mighty jump and whirled sharply to the left. The rider leaned so far to the left that someone said his left ear scraped up some dirt, but he stayed on. The crowd was back of the local cowpoke. They were hoping that he would show the professionals that he could ride, too. But it was not to be. Two more quick whirls and a sharp jump, and the

rider went sailing over the horse's head.

"Six and one-half seconds."

The horse's owner figured that the horse had had enough.

"The show is over," she said as she started to lead the horse away. By now, the crowd was getting ugly again. Her husband tried to stop her, but with no success. Others were begging her not to take the horse away.

She stopped when Johnny Muir came over. He stroked the horse's head and neck, calming it down. He smiled at the lady.

"The horse is fine," he said. "In fact, he seems to be enjoying it more than the riders are."

This didn't set too well with the local buckaroos. They descended on her, demanding that she let Johnny Muir try to ride him.

"No," she said. It was obvious she was getting angry. "My horse has thrown enough drunken buckaroos for one day."

"The big shot from Pendleton isn't drunk," one loud-mouthed cowpoke shouted with his face directly in front of hers. "I dare you to let him try to ride."

Johnny Muir came to the lady's defense, asking them to quiet down.

"I'll be glad to ride him, but only if the lady asks me to."

The crowd turned on her again, begging her to let Johnny have a ride.

"All right," she finally agreed. She then spoke directly to Johnny. "But, remember, no spurs."

Johnny looked over at Old Nelson who nodded and held up the $25 ride money promised to the Pendleton rider. Johnny sent for his saddle. When it came, he took his time and cinched it just the way he wanted it. While this was going on, we could hear bets being made all through the crowd. Just as Johnny was ready to mount, the spokesman for the local buckaroos asked him to wait. Calling some of his buddies aside, he proposed that they raise $25 and bet it against Johnny. The money was quickly raised, and he approached the Pendleton rider.

"Here's twenty-five dollars that we'll bet against your ride money," the local cowpoke said. "Is it a bet?"

Johnny hesitated before answering.

"On one condition," he said. "If I am thrown, I get a second chance."

The angry crowd immediately hooted down Johnny's suggestion.

"All right," Johnny said. "It's a bet, but I want to see the money in Mr. Nelson's hand before the ride starts."

When Old Nelson had the buckaroos' money, he held it up for Johnny to see; and Johnny swung up into the saddle.

The horse immediately went into his routine of mixing hard, fast jumps with quick whirls. But he couldn't unseat the stubborn rider.

"Five seconds," Old Nelson called.
"Ten seconds."
"Fifteen seconds."
"Twenty seconds."

Then the horse stopped with his head between his forelegs. Johnny reached down, stroked the gallant horse's neck and spoke calmly to the wild-eyed animal. The horse gradually reacted to Johnny's soft treatment.

In the meantime, arguements were starting in the crowd. Those who had bet on Johnny were claiming the ride was over and wanted to collect their bets. Others disagreed. They were still hoping that the horse would dump Johnny. Finally, Johnny pulled up the horse's head and stepped down from the saddle. The local loud-mouth immediately shouted that Johnny had lost the bet.

Johnny paid no attention to the loud-mouth's claims. He tested the cinch and tightened it slightly before swinging easily back into the saddle.

He turned the horse toward the wild bunch of horses on the far side of the pasture. The big horse bolted toward them, and Johnny let him run until the two mounted riders helped him turn the horse back toward the crowd.

About halfway back, the horse stopped. He had rested and looked like he was ready to buck again. Johnny let him rest and, standing up in the stirrups, began to sing *Home on the Range*. The crowd didn't seem to appreciate Johnny's showmanship.

Suddenly, Johnny took off his big hat, hit the horse on the rump with it and dug his heels (minus spurs) into the horse's ribs. This was the signal for the horse to begin bucking and sunfishing harder than ever. And, while the horse was doing its best to unseat him, Johnny was still singing *Home on the Range* at the top of his voice.

When the heaving horse finally gave up, Johnny rode him back to the crowd and stopped in front of Old Nelson.

"Did I win the bet?"
"You sure did."

Johnny stepped down from the horse and took the $50 from Nelson. He then led the horse back to the lady and stood there, calming him with his soothing voice. He continued bragging on the horse and offered to continue breaking it into a top riding animal. She thanked him and invited him to visit her and her husband if he was ever in the Powell Butte area.

Johnny removed his saddle and handed the reins to her husband who asked one of the riders to take the horse back to the buggy which was parked under a tree.

The bunch of local buckaroos were suddenly quiet. The reason was soon apparant. They had taken the horse away from the rider who was returning it to the buggy and put another saddle on it. The local loud-mouth was in the saddle, spurring the horse mercilessly trying to make it buck again.

The horse responded — only too well. Three big jumps, and the loud-mouth sailed high and far over the horse's head, striking the ground with a thud as he lay still.

The horse's owner was furious.

She grabbed a quirt from a bystander and ran to the fallen cowpoke who was just then struggling to regain his feet. She lashed him several times with the quirt as the rider tried in vain to protect himself.

In the meantime, the local cowpoke's girl friend took offense at the beating her boy friend was receiving. She grabbed the lady from behind, ripping off about half of her white shirtwaist.

This was the spark that set the crowd on fire. What had been a good, old-fashioned, country get-together suddenly became a riot. Long dormant petty jealousies and personal dislikes came alive in the rough-and-tumble combat. Even motherly housewives were drawn into the melee when they would rush in to protect a member of their family. Youngsters who became enraged at the sight of a father or older brother being whipped rushed into the fight only to be confronted by another of their age and size.

The sudden sight of his wife's bare shoulders sobered the Powell Butte rancher quickly. He rushed to help her, taking off his shirt to cover her. But, as his hands were behind his back trying to remove the shirt, someone gave him a violent shove and he went sprawling onto the ground.

Old Nelson was doing his best to stop the riot. He would get one fight stopped, but two more would start in its place. His biggest worry was firearms. He knew many of the men in the fight were armed; and, if one shot was fired, it could set off a disasterous chain of events.

Johnny Muir and Billy Wray missed the beginning of the free-for-all, because they had carried Johnny's saddle back to the truck. Hearing the uproar, they hurried back and joined the baseball players who were perfectly willing to watch the activities from the sidelines. They seemed to enjoy the action and were reluctant to go. Old Nelson came over and urged all of us to leave the area. He was afraid that the crowd would turn on Johnny and Billy.

So Johnny Muir and Billy Wray drove away in their truck and headed back to Pendleton. The defeated Henry's Mill baseball team headed east across the big flats toward logging country.

A couple of days later, Gene Phillips who had a homestead not far from the mill showed up with a beautiful black eye. Nobody asked him about it, and he volunteered no information.

Looking backward over some 63 years, I'll have to say that, when Alkali Flat has a Fourth of July celebration, it's a lulu.

What had been a good, old-fashioned, country get-together suddenly became a riot.

The Mystery of Oregon's Displaced Birds

By Gladyn Condor

A strange noise awakened us one cold, snowy morning in 1970 at Bar Dough Brand Ranch in Long Valley, Idaho. Having lived there seven years, we readily recognized every individual bark, yap, grunt, howl, whistle and call customarily made by our wildlife neighbors, both furred and feathered. But this raucous noise was like none we had ever heard. Even Shane, our shepherd-wolf dog, a somewhat "second cousin" to some of these wild critters, was aroused.

"What do you think it is?" I asked Dave, my husband, as we climbed out of bed and rushed into the kitchen, donning our robes as we ran.

Long Valley snuggled between lofty ranges of the Rocky Mountains and backed up against Idaho's Primitive Area. The winters here were long and hard. Deep snow, at times, made it impossible for wild creatures to find food. So, each year, we set-up food-stations — one in a meadow behind our house and the other, a bird-feeder, kept well-filled with suet on the back-yard fence. Both were visible from our kitchen windows.

It was still several hours before daylight and quite dark outside. The wind, howling like a demented banshee, swirled heavily falling snow furiously about, greatly impairing our vision from our kitchen windows. The sound appeared to be coming from the back-fence feeder. Still, we could not be sure the visitors were birds.

This wasn't the first time we had been awakened by an unexpected "guest." One night, a young cougar, much to his mother's frustration, decided to sample our suet. Proving too large for the feeder-trays, the young cougar had plummeted with a yowl to the ground, taking much of the bird-feeder with him.

Was some strange critter again caught in our bird-feeder?

Between gusts of wind-blown snow, we could catch glimpses of flying objects fluttering and swooping about the feeder. They seemed larger than the birds in our area. And no call we had ever heard compared with the sound

those creatures were making.

"Beats me what they are," Dave finally got around to replying. He busied himself for a moment getting the coffee on. "Guess we'll just have to wait until daylight to see what's happening out there."

As daylight came, we discovered we had been invaded by a host of strange birds built like small crows. But they were a light gray color — not black.

How many? That was a good question. Birds filled the feeder, birds clustered together in a group on the snow-covered ground, and an undeterminable number fluttered

One of the "lost" nutcrackers. Photo was taken through kitchen window.

impatiently around the feeder. Apparently, our supply of suet had been depleted long before their ravenous appetites had been satiated. They were making known their plight with their gutteral, grating caws. They could be heard above the loud howl of the wind.

"Something mighty strange has happened," Dave said as he reached for the telephone. "We need help. I'm calling Charlie and Steve up at the Wildlife Service Office."

Fortunately, Charlie had come into the Cascade (Idaho) office early that

morning. Admitting he could not identify the birds from Dave's description, he did agree to get Steve and come to our ranch as soon as possible. And he also promised to bring along all of the suet they could find.

The birds seemed to sense that the Wildlife truck's arrival meant a new supply of food. They retreated — cautiously, but not fearfully — a short distance from the feeder. Gathered together on the ground, the cawing birds watched intently as the men refilled the feeder and strung suet on the fence. Hardly waiting for the men to leave, the birds descended en masse, like a bunch of scavengers on a fresh kill.

Steve took a Polaroid photograph of them to take back to the office for identification. Their bodies were a light gray, as we had said, with black wings and tail. Large white patches on their wings and tail, shown on the photograph, conclusively identified them, according to Steve's Wildlife Chart, as Nutcrackers.

Mounting a camera on a telescope-tripod which we kept by the window to more closely study our daily guests to our feeding-stations, we tried taking a photograph. Despite the lack of light due to the continuing snowfall, we managed to obtain one quite good photograph. And, adding more veracity to the bird's identification was the chart's technical description of the bird's call, terming it a "flat, grating caw — a KHRAA." This was most definitely the sound that had haunted us since long before daylight that morning.

No wonder we had not recognized the birds. They were not indigenous to our locale. They were a long way from "home." The Nutcracker's normal habitat is in Oregon, in the great Basin of the Rocky Mountains and between the Coastal Range and the Cascade-Sierras. They inhabit the high mountains, near timberline, along this basin and range from Canada to Baja California.

How had they gotten so far away from their home territory? That was as much a mystery to our local Wildlife officers as to us. And how were we going to care for this flock of strange birds?

Luckily, the birds seemed content to gorge themselves on our suet. Surely, it was far from their normal diet. But keeping an adequate supply of suet to satisfy their seeming voracious appetites would be a monumental task.

Having proved to his satisfaction that the birds were Oregon Nutcrackers, Steve decided to call the Wildlife Office in Boise for assistance.

"Boy, are we in luck!" he said as he turned away from the telephone. "A team of Wildlife Officers and a Meteorologist were heading this way from Boise. Their office reached them by radio. They'll be here in about an hour. Oh, yes, I asked them to find some more suet."

There was nothing more we could do but wait. Dave and Shane went out for their morning walk. I started breakfast for the two men and us. Apparently satisfied for the moment, the birds had flown over to a large stand of Ponderosas and Cedars bordering the east side of our meadow. Their loud cawing was still clearly heard.

The two Wildlife Officers and the Meteorologist arrived. All were most curious about the strange birds. The Meteorologist, Jim Bradley, had a personal interest.

"I knew my theory of the 'red snow' was correct," he said. "And, now, the old Jet Stream has done it again . . . dumping a flock of displaced birds on your ranch."

"Red snow? Birds 'dumped' by the Jet Stream? What are you talking about?"

"I'm talking about those birds out there," Bradley said slowly. "How do you think they got here if not on the Jet Stream?"

"Are we on a Jet Stream course?" Dave asked.

"Yes, a northerly branch."

Bradley laid out a world map on the table and began tracing the Jet Stream's course.

"The Jet Stream generally follows the 30th parallel," he said, pointing to the map. "It swings eastward from the Pacific Ocean here near the United States—Mexico border, flows across the southern part of the United States, over Florida's northern border, then back out over the Atlantic. Continuing on its eastward course, it flows over Russia, North Africa and mainland China, completely circling the hemisphere before repeating its swing back across the Pacific to the North American continent."

He went on to explain how the Jet Stream — an erratic, meandering river of air — flows in the 10,000 to 40,000 foot altitude range and has a marked influence on storms, even local climates. While the velocity of the Jet Stream may

Our strange, unexpected guests — "blown in" by a fluke of Nature — had flown out, guided by their natural homing instincts. They had made our winter eventful by their presence.

vary, the winds remain amazingly constant in their west-to-east direction around the globe.

However, the Jet Stream frequently branches into several narrow streams of air, and its course varies with a northward swing in winter and a southward course in summer.

"As the Stream's currents sweep across the Pacific Ocean over the Japanese current, they often scoop up heavily moisture-laden warm air currents. Frequently foreign material, carried on lesser wind currents, is caught in an up-draft and carried aloft into the Jet Stream current. In this case, it was Oregon Nutcrackers which were sucked into the Jet Stream's swirling currents."

Agian, he turned back to the map . . .

"But, as the Jet Stream sweeps northward, it has to rise to go over the Continental Divide — which is close-by your ranch — and its warm moist air chills and turns to snow, a cargo too heavy for the Stream to carry. So it simply dumps the snow and whatever else it's carrying — in this case, birds."

"Could that explain the Ginger blossom aroma we often smell after a storm?" I asked. "The fragrance-laden warm air becomes perfumed snow?"

Bradley nodded.

"Precisely. In 1959 — quite near here

— a fresh snowfall was bright red instead of white. Analyzation showed that the coloring was red dye. Its source was not made known. But U.S. investigators were convinced that a foreign country was experimenting with the Jet Stream's potential as a carrier . . . perhaps for germ warfare."

It was dreadful to contemplate. And, later, the U.S. Department of State did disclose that, in 1970 (the year our bird "dumping" occurred), the Soviets were found to be operating germ warfare plants along the Aral Sea in Russia. Alledgedly, the United States was to be the target of "experiments" with the Jet Stream as a carrier of "flu" germs.

According to authorative government medical reports, a flu virus of unidentified variety did hit Idaho, Colorado and Wyoming in 1973 and in 1974. (Our family was affected by the 1973 epidemic.) A similar flu struck mainland China in 1975 causing many casualties. In 1976, also with fatal results, flu afflicted residents of Mexico. In 1977, (the year President Ford frantically called for mass "flu immunization"), the Jet Stream went berserk, veering further south than ever before, causing terrible storms. Finally, a flu virus that affected southern U.S. residents in 1978 was publicly verified by the Communicable Disease Center at Atlanta, Georgia, as being "Russian flu."

To be sure, no Governmental communiques were ever published confirming the Soviets as perpetrators of these flu epidemics. Yet there were authentic State Department reports confirming the existence of germ warfare plants in Russia. All of the countries affected were on the Jet Stream's course. Furthermore, the mysterious arrival of the Oregon birds had now, without a doubt, proved the Jet Stream's phenomenal capability as a carrier.

Thanks to contributions of suet by neighboring ranches and local meat markets, our Nutcrackers survived the winter. In the spring, they nested in conifer trees and raised their young. As fall approached, their restlessness became obvious. Then, suddenly, like the migration of geese, the Nutcrackers swarmed into the sky, heading "home." We never saw any of them again.

Our strange, unexpected guests — "blown in " by a fluke of Nature had flown out, guided by their natural homing instincts. They had made our winter eventful by their presence. Their arrival had proved the Jet Stream's capability as a carrier.

Indeed, Oregon's Nutcrackers had made history and had helped prove a technological theory, as well — the night they unintentionally rode the Jet Stream from Oregon into Idaho.

No. 14

The Mystery of the Lost Crystal Cave

By Patti D. Wood

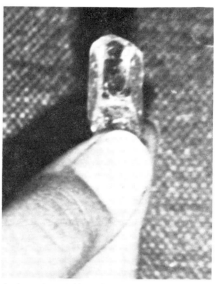

A piece of crystal from the cave folks have been in search of for nearly 75 years. Why? Because its worth is estimated in the millions.   Photo by Brad Simpson

The year was 1904.

The desert southeast of Bend was little different from what it is today. Scattered clumps of sagebrush, and a few stunted junipers. But, for the most part, it was the same then as it is today . . . miles and miles of nothing.

The only sign of life in that great expanse was a column of dust moving slowly westward in the vicinity of Pine Mountain. It was a cattledrive - on its way from the Burns area to the LaPine area.

Driving slow-moving cattle was hot, man-killing work. When the drive boss passed the word for the men to bed down for the night, he didn't have to say it twice. The trail hands were hot, dusty, and hungry, and they looked forward to a good, hot supper and a night's sleep.

While some of the men took care of the needs of the cattle, others went out and gathered wood. You couldn't cook supper without firewood, and it took a lot of walking to find relatively little wood in the sparse vegetation of the Oregon desert, so the wood gatherers spread out. Soon, one of them shouted into the evening's silence.

"Hey, fellas! Look what I found!"

Curiosity won out over hunger, and they hurried over to the man who had called out.

"What is it?"

"Looks like a cave opening."

He pointed to a narrow opening near a jutting rock ledge. He stooped over to peer inside.

"It's darker than Grandma's cellar down there!"

One of them picked up a rock and tossed it into the opening. From the hollow sound of the falling stone, it was apparent that there was a sizeable cavern beyond the opening.

"Wonder what's in it?"

"Dunno. But I'm sure gonna find out. Anybody want to come with me?"

"Sure!"

Every one of the cowpunchers volunteered to explore the cave.

They fashioned a torch from a small juniper limb one of them was carrying. Before long, it was putting out smoky but sufficient light.

"Gimme the torch. I'll go first."

The volunteer took the torch and carefully lowered himself through the narrow opening.

"What do you see?"

"My God! You'll never believe it!"

"What is it?"

"You'll have to see for yourself."

One by one, the men lowered themselves into the cave's darkness until they were all inside.

"Well, will you look at that?" gasped a man as he surveyed the view. The light from the torch was reflected from the walls and ceiling in the form of thousands of tiny pinpoints of light which glistened and sparkled, giving the cave's interior a mysterious quality. It was several seconds before any of them spoke.

"What is it? Diamonds?"

"Naw. Never heard of diamonds anywhere in this country."

One of the men broke off a piece of the reflecting substance and held it under the flickering torch.

"It's some kind of crystal. There must be tons of it."

"It's spooky in here, I'm gettin' outta here."

"I am, too. But I'm gonna pick up some of the stuff first."

Several of the cowpunchers took samples of the crystals before returning to the fading daylight to continue their wood collecting.

When the cowpunchers arrived in Bend, they entertained the patrons of the local saloon with stories of their marvelous find in the desert. And they showed their pieces of crystal to back up their story. Even so, few people believed them. A few of the sample crystals changed hands over drinks; and, within a few days, the wild tale had spread all through the town.

One man in Bend was not so sure the story of the crystal cave was a hoax. He was Nicholas Paul Smith, owner of the old Smith's Hardware store on Wall Street. Nick Smith was, perhaps, a little better educated than his contemporaries. When he came into possession of some of the crystals, he decided to investigate the tale. He packed some food and headed his horse toward Pine Mountain to try to pick up the trail of the cattle drive.

For more than 20 years, Nick Smith tried without success to relocate the crystal cave where he once had explored and removed crystals.

Marjorie Smith was ten years old when her father located the cave. She has two pieces of the crystal, which is kept in a bank deposit box.

According to an account of Smith's search by a man named Merle Jones, it was late afternoon of the third day when Nick located the cattledrive's trail. A short time later, he found the small cave opening and prepared to explore it. He entered the cave and gathered up a number of crystals, gaping at the sparkling shadows his torch created on the walls and ceiling. Soon though, he was forced to abandon his exploration because of an approaching snowstorm.

As Nick rode back toward Bend, he was confident that he could return to the cave when he wanted. When he returned to Bend, he contacted "Aunt Moll" Nichols in Tumlalo. A woman with a noticeably unique character, Aunt Moll was considered to be a reputable authority on rocks. When Nick showed her the crystal samples he had removed from the cave, she readily agreed to accompany him on a return trip to the cave in the spring.

When Nick and Aunt Moll rode out the following spring, all traces of the cattle trail had been erased by the snow and winds of the harsh winter. Everything seemed unfamiliar. Nick failed to recognize any of the landmarks he had so carefully noted on his first trip. The desert wasteland had apparently disguised the cave opening, leaving it undetectable.

For the next 20 years, Nick rode out on the desert in search of the lost cave. Others have searched for it, but in vain, as the cave remains lost today.

The cave was found on two separate occasions - once by the cattlemen and once by Nick Smith - almost 75 years ago. The only clue to its whereabouts is that it is "somewhere southeast of Millican in the vicinity of Pine Mountain."

As Central Oregon residents and visitors know, the Oregon desert is, for the most part, barren and dry. It will require a considerable amount of luck to find the cave's entrance. Yet, an estimate of the cave's value runs at the million dollar mark.

Nick's daughter, Marjorie, lives in Bend and still has two of the crystals said to have come from the lost cave. She keeps them in a bank deposit box, removing them only to be photographed.

"What are the crystals worth?" was a natural question.

"I have no idea," she answers. "As far as I am concerned, they are my personal treasures — part of my inheritance. They were so much a part of my father's life that I wouldn't part with them under any circumstances."

"What if the cave should be found again? Who would own the crystals?"

"I'm not sure," she said. "I think my father had a deed to the land, but it was destroyed when the old Bend courthouse burned a number of years ago. The Bureau of Land Management now owns the land, and I believe it would become a famous tourist attraction."

"I wish I could remember more, but I was so young at the time. My father had an exceptional sense of direction, but sand and sagebrush must have buried the cave's opening. Dad made trips out there for 20 years or so, often staying out in the desert for as long as two weeks searching for it. It's just lost."

Marjorie told me about one young man who spent an entire summer making a systematic search of the entire area. He divided the area into small squares and closely searched each one. He was very confident in the beginning and promised her that he would find the lost cave.

"I never heard from him after he gave up on the search."

The area is dotted with numerous lava caves, and discovery of these has no doubt lifted the hopes of searchers momentarily. But the real crystal cave has never been found.

Other caves — some of great scientific interest — have been discovered in the area. One of them is the unique Lavacicle Cave. Inside Lavacicle Cave are thousands of stalactites and stalagmits formed of lava. Partially because of its scientific value and because of vandalism, the Forest Service has built steel gates to keep people out. Lavacicle Cave may be visited only on guided tours.

Geologists have speculated that, if there is a crystal cave, it would likely be located at the junction of the lava lands (around Pine Mountain) and former marine formations (Dry River, Horse Ridge area).

This story has been told and retold for almost 75 years. It is reasonable to assume that certain facts have been distorted, so that now it is difficult to separate fact from fiction.

Yet many feel that the crystals Marjorie Smith has in her possession offer real and tangible proof. Others believe that the crystal cave never existed.

One thing remains a certainty. The mystery of lost crystal cave remains as much a mystery in 1979 as it was in 1904. But who knows? You may be the one to find it and settle the argument once and for all.

Good luck!

It will require a considerable amount of luck to find the cave's entrance. Yet, an estimate of the cave's value runs at the million dollar mark.

Historic Sunriver Meadow

During World War II this symbolic log structure stood at the entrance to U.S. Army Engineers Camp Abbot, a training center which covered a sizeable part of what is now Sunriver.

By Thomas J. Lewis

The meadow at Sunriver Resort was known to the beaver trappers in 1825 as the "Canoe Camp," and in 1853, it was a campsite used by the McClure-Bond wagons traveling upriver searching for the new Free Emigrant Road, the terminus of the Middle Emigrant Route across Central Oregon's High Desert region to the Willamette Valley.

Nearby Sunriver Meadow is the old ford used by Lt. John C. Fremont's exploration party in the Winter of 1843. West of the Deschutes River was the ancient Indian trail to the Columbia River used by Lt. Henry Abbot with Lt. Robert Williamson's Pacific Railroad Survey party, assisted by two other lieutenants who would later become general, Philip Sheridan and George Crook.

In 1904, the site of Sunriver Meadow was sold for $2,300 by James Pelton of Klamath Falls to Fred A. Shonquest, who operated a ranch on "Shonquest Meadow."

During World War II, Camp Abbot was constructed at a cost of over $4 million on the Meadow as an Engineer Replacement Center. It opened in May, 1943, to accommodate ten thousand soldiers. After operating only a year, the buildings were all razed, except for the log building called the Great Hall today, which served then as the Officer's Club. Afterwards the Meadow was acquired by the Hudspeth Land and Livestock Co. of Prineville.

Camp Abbot was an operational center for the "Oregon Maneuver" war-game training exercises in 1943 involving over 100,000 soldiers of the IV Army Corps, commanded by Major General Alexander M. Patch, including the 91st, 96th, and 104th Infantry Divisions, and General George Patton's tank units.

On November 16, 1826, Hudson Bay Co. beaver trappers led by Peter Skene Ogden discovered Paulina and East Lakes in Newberry Crater, and he noted in his journal: "It was a consolation to see our poor horses quench their thirst." By the next day, Ogden had reached the Little Deschutes near present La Pine, and on the following day camped in today's Sunriver Meadow, where the previous year trappers Tom McKay and Finan McDonald built canoes to descent the "Riviere des Chutes"

("River of the Ripids" or "Falls River") to the French-Canadian voyageurs. On arriving at the "Canoe Encampment," Ogden wrote: "Thank God. The road to the Clammitte (Klamaths) we all know."

A son of trapper Tom McKay (pronounced Mac-Kie) visited his father's old "Canoe Camp" 42-years later, while leading some Warm Springs Indian Scouts during Lieutenant Colonel George Crook's Army Campaign against the renegade Paiutes. Traveling 16-miles in 4½-hours from his previous camp near Crescent, a little below the junction of the Klamath and Eugene Roads, Dr. William McKay wrote on September 23, 1867, after arriving at Sunriver Meadow:

"...traveled down the DeChutes to the Canoe Encampment...beautiful road, more mud than usual at this season of the year. Elegant camp, abundance of grass of the best quality. Everybody went out fishing & caught about 300 lbs. of trout.

Tuesday, 24. Left camp at 10 to 7 O'clock. Traveled round the Lava Butte, traveled till noon...and

---

EDITOR'S NOTE: Historian Tom Lewis is Teamster and Wagon Master at Sunriver Resort's Stables with his Morgan team from the Oregon Wagon of the Bicentennial Wagon Train Pilgrimage to Pennsylvania, along the Oregon Trail, via the Barlow Wagon Road around Mt. Hood,(or the Northern Emigrant Route). They also traveled together by covered wagon over the Southern Emigrant Route, called the Applegate Trail in 1846, on another Bicentennial Wagon Train trek from the Klamath basin across the Siskiyous to the historic mining town of Jacksonville in 1976.

One of the wagons from the Bicentennial Wagon Train Pilgrimage to Pennsylvania. Here they ford the John Day River in eastern Oregon.

camped on the first water at DeChutes at Tamolowa (mouth of Tumalo Creek). Traveled 18 miles.

In the winter of 1843, Army explorer John C. Fremont led a party up the Deschutes into California, guided by scout Kit Carson. At the request of the Methodist Missionary, Fremont left The Dalles with an Indian lad named Billy Chinook, the 19-year old son of a Wasco Chief, who wanted to "see the whites." Fremont took young Billy East to Washington, D.C., and to Philadelphia, where he attended schools and learned English fluently, and returned West again with Fremont. Billy signed the 1855 Treaty creating the Warm Springs Reservation for the Middle Oregon Tribes. In 1866-7, he was among the Warm Springs Indians serving as Army Scouts assigned to Cpt. John Darragh's company, not with McKay's Deschutes warriors (enlistment officer Lt. Borrowe learned that the Warm Springs "tribes are very clanish, not intermingling in any way.") In 1864 he was credited with killing Tam-ow-ins, the medicine man who made charms supposed to provide Chief Paulina with invulnerability to white man's bullets.

Fremont forded the Deschutes River just north of Sunriver Meadow, about 15-miles from upper Paulina Creek, a location associated with Paulina's band of Snakes. To the Indians along the Columbia, the Deschutes River was known as the "Sho-sho-ne" or Snake Indian River. Fremont referred to the numerous Paiute, or "digger" Indians of the Malheur-Harney basin, as the most primitive of any humans he had ever seen. They had a wild appearance, acted impulsively without much forethought, and their main preoccupation was food gathering for survival in the arid, desert terrain.

In 1853, the largest of all wagon trains to use the Middle Emigrant Route, 250 wagons and 1,027 persons, plus stock, were guided by Elijah Elliott to Lane County and Eugene City over the Willamette Pass near Diamond Peak, following the Middle Fork of the Willamette River. Elliott's Cutoff party followed the tracks left in 1845 by the famous "Lost Wagon Train" of Blue Bucket Gold fame, led first into Central Oreon's High Desert region by Stephen Meek, along the Malheur River to Harney Lake route followed by the fur trappers to the Snake River from the confluence of the Crooked River with the Deschutes near Madras.

In his diary, Andrew S. McClure recorded the suffering crossing 75-mile and 50-mile deserts between Harney Lake and the Deschutes River near Bend. Another McClure, James, also kept a journal, writing on October 7, 1853: "Fall River, a beautiful stream 50 yards wide." He also added: "The desert we have just crossed is covered with the finest kind of bunch grass." J. Marion Gale described the arrival at the Deschutes River in the vicinity of Bend.

"That day about 150 wagons, with almost famished teams and immigrants, camped on the banks of the rapid, sparkling river and drank of its waters, more delicious than wine, to our satisfaction; and never in my life have I seen a day so intensely enjoyed in drinking as was that to us and our poor beasts.

In the meantime, scouts had gone ahead on horseback to seek the new road, and after a number of days delay and perplexing search it was found about thirty miles from this camp."

Most of the Elliott wagons rounded Lava Butte, camping near the Deschutes River in the vicinity of Sunriver Meadow, and then travelled southward on the east side of the Little Deschutes, through land homesteaded in 1878 by William P. and Grace Clark Vandervert, crossing the Deschutes near Crescent, at the head of the newly blazed "Free Emigrant Road." Some emigrants also forded the Deschutes River about where the Colonel Besson Bridge once stood, just downstream from Besson campground boat ramp, the pioneers then travelling south along the west side of the Deschutes presumably along the ancient trail to the Columbia River used by the "Marsh People" of the Klamath Lake region. Today, visitors at Sunriver Resort's stables can enjoy covered wagon tours and hayrides to a shady picnic area adjacent to the site of the bridge named for Camp Abbot Commander, Colonel Frank S. Besson. Where covered wagons once forded, now the osprey, heron, hawks, and eagles hunt fish, and canoes float by quietly.

BIBLIOGRAPHY

Brogan, Phil, **East of the Cascades,** 1977.

Clark, Keith and Donna, "William McKay's Journal 1866-67; Indian Scouts," **Oregon Historical Quarterly,** Summer and Fall, 1978

Menefee, Leah Collins, and Lowell Tiller, "Cutoff Fever," **Oregon Historical Quarterly,** September and December, 1977.

In his diary, Andrew S. McClure recorded the suffering crossing 75-mile and 50-mile deserts between Harney Lake and the Deschutes River near Bend.

Little Known Tales from Oregon History

Driving Lumbe

No. 15

by Dean Hollinshead

When I was a young man, in 1917, I lived at LaPine, Oregon with not much work to do, but seemed to always have a job when I wanted one. I drove solid tired trucks for my brother Chit Hollinshead, I'd build rail fences or most anything I could to make a few dollars.

One day I was at LaPine, sitting on the sidewalk as most of us did when we didn't have anything to do, just putting in the time, when I looked down the road toward Bend, and there came a big, four horse team pulling a logging wagon with two more big horses tied on behind.

I got real excited about the outfit coming toward us, for I really hadn't seen six beautiful horses that were coming my way.

I said "Oh boy, look at those horses." And the gang said, "Yeah, horses, so what." I soon told them that they had never seen horses like that in their whole life, which was sure true.

The driver drove 'em up and stopped. I ran out and said, "Oh boy, what beautiful horses, where in 'ell are you going with 'em?"

He said, "I am going to the Master Saw Mill, could you tell me which way to go?"

I said I could tell him all right, but that mill is not running and hasn't been for some time.

He said the IXL Lumber Company from Bend was going to start it up and he was going to do the logging for them.

I told him which way to go and it was about seven or eight miles on up the river, "You can't miss the place because there was only one other place on that road and it belonged to my dad, and I'm going home pretty soon, and if you have any trouble I will help ya out."

"I got a Model T sittin' right there and if you don't go too fast, I might catch up." "You will catch me all right!" He said, "I only make about three miles per hour."

I fooled around town for two or three hours and got into "Old Lizzy" and headed for home at my dad's place, and you know what? I never did catch up with him that night. I got all hopped up the next morning, and Dad and I got into "Old Lizzy" and rattled off up to the Master Saw Mill.

When we got there, we were surprised to find out that Elmer Merrell, who was a good friend of my dads and Mr. Wilcox, who we didn't know, was the IXL Lumber Company.

Mr. Master, who owned and ran the mill when it did run, was shipping his lumber to Bend by solid tired trucks. My brother had some of them trucks, but it didn't seem to pay, hauling the lumber by truck. This new company was going to cut the lumber, put it on two wheeled dollies and push it on a plank tram to the river, which was only about two hundred feet, and dump it in the river. Away it would go down the Little Deschutes, into the Big Deschutes, and on down to

Benham Falls. Then they'd take that lumber out of the river, load it on trucks and haul it the rest of the way. This was a sure cheap, easier way to get this lumber hauled about twenty five miles closer to Bend. The bad part of this was the lumber would not float. Most of it went right to the bottom of the Little Deschutes, and what did float, ran up in the willows and jammed the river for about two miles before they, the IXL Lumber Company, decided it couldn't be done that way. This is where the fun and the work began. The logging outfit was working fine, hauling nice big yellow pine logs, more than the mill could cut per day. The mill was putting out about twelve to fifteen thousand hard foot per day, but they had the tie-up at the river.

I went up there most every day and watched the operation and talked to Elmer Merrell, who was pretty much down in spirits.

He said to me one day, "Dean, you are about the longest thing we got around here, do you think you could clear the river so we could get rafts of lumber thru there?" I said, "I don't know anything about being a river rat, but I can wade out as far as any one else can, and I do want a job."

Here is where the fun started. We had one small boat, with motor, that could keep you from drowning, if it got there quick enough. They sent all the mill crew out with me and the boat. We started on the lumber jam farthest from the mill and we broke it

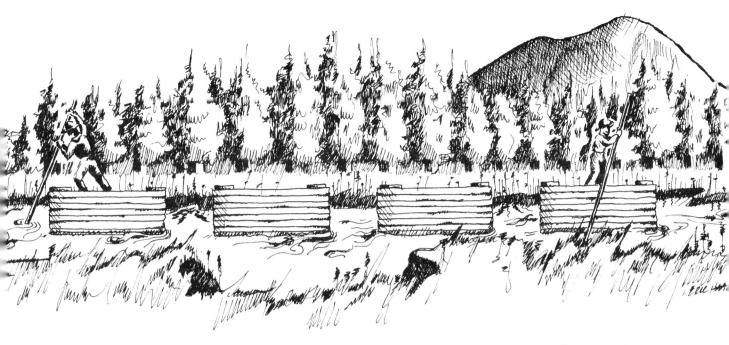

Down the Deschutes on Rafts

loose, which took two men. Down the river a little way, the rest of the men fixed a set of skids on the bank of the river, two big logs well anchored on the bank with the other end in the river and as the lumber came down, these men would pick up each board and lay it on the skids until they had a raft of about one thousand feet of lumber. Then they bolted it together with two cross ties at each end, then they'd push it out in the river and tie up. Then they'd do the same thing again.

We would put forty-two of these rafts together in line down the river and take off for Benham Falls. There were three of us on each string.

Then they fastened these together with a 2 x 12, with a bolt in each end thru the top cross tie, that way they were all tied together but they all had a chance to bend or swing as we went down the river around all the crooked bends. Take a good look at the pictures to see how crooked the Little Deschutes River really is.

It took about a week for the six of us to finish out the first string. We were wet all day long, we had to wade in water up to our belts and if you stepped into a hole, you had to chase your hat down river until you caught up with it. We had lots of fun watching the other guy fall in but when it came to your turn it sometimes wasn't that funny.

At last the big day rolled around to start the first string down that awful crooked river. Take another good look

This aerial view shows how the Little Deschutes winds and creates many challenges for inexperienced river rats.   Dave Swan Photo

at the pictures and you can see what we were up against. We started out with Mr. Swayze, myself and a man called Bill, I have forgotten his last name, but we three stayed together most all summer.

We turned the string loose, hoping for the best, but it didn't happen that way.

We found out, but quick, that the tail raft would travel about three times as fast as the lead raft would, so we tied up again and fixed a brake on the back raft.

We had to rebuild the back raft so we could drag a big pole on the bottom of the river, but still stick up high enough for one man to operate. We loosened up the bolts that held the raft together and pushed the lumber in the middle of the raft until we had about a three foot slot in the back of the raft. Then we bolted a 2 x 6 across the back of the hole and a loose 2 x 6 on the front of the hole so we could put our brake pole thru the hole until one end dragged on the bottom of the river, which would slow the raft down until everything was straight, then take out the loose 2 x 6. The pole would fly up and fall on the raft and away we go until some one called for the brake. Mr. Swayze was the braker and Bill and I tried to get the string around the bends of the river.

We got along pretty good the first day but we sure had a lot to learn. We found out there were lots of sand bars running out in the river on most all

*We would put
forty-two of these
rafts together in a
line down the river
and take off for
Benham Falls.*

the turns and the string would not float over the bars and everything would stop, Swayze would put on the brake to hold the floaters back while Bill and I would try to get off the bar, that was a lot of work. We weren't straight enough to get the raft off the sand bar and keep the next one from coming in on the same bar, so we just sat down and looked at all those rafts we had to get thru, all at once I had an idea, I said, "Bill, let's turn the lead raft crosswise in the current of the river and stand on the up-river side and see if we can sink the raft up edge-wise." So at it we went, we got it crosswise and stood on the up-river side in water up to our belts, and sometimes more, you would not guess how much power we got by just standing there, but we had plenty power to pull Mr. Sand Bar right on down the river with us, if one raft wouldn't pull the load, we would sink two rafts and that way we didn't have to worry about power. Swayze would pull his brake and away we would go again.

Most of the time we could keep the string going, unless we ran into a real bad place, but it was hard work all the time.

We had all of our camp outfit with us; beds, grub and cooking utensils. When night came, we could get along fine.

It was during war times, in 1917, when you couldn't buy food very easy. We were always short of bread, flour, bacon, eggs and so on. As we drifted down river, if there was a ranch in sight, Bill or I would jump off the raft and beg for anything we could get, mostly bread, they were all very good by giving us anything they had that we could eat.

We were mostly alone on these trips for no one knew for sure where we were. Of course we could always walk up to the Bend road if we got in a jam.

After about the second or third day, we knew how to get along better and we traveled faster. About our third day out we are going along fine, we have made about seven land miles, and of course, I don't know how many river miles, but probably around 25 to 30.

We have gone under two bridges and several real bad places, but we still have the lead raft in front and the rear raft in the back, with good old Swayze and his trusty brake. As I said before, we couldn't go without him, and being willing to do as Bill and I ask him to do, he was some man, believe me.

We hit good water lots of places and we would make good time, then bang,

a sunken log or something in the river we didn't see, so we might be held up there for most of a day and night. We seemed to be able to get loose some way. As the rafts drifted down the river, it seemed like it got easier to control them, so we made good time. We went by several ranches, the Frank Bogue Ranch, Pengry Ranch, and when we got to the Bill Bogue ranch, my partner Bill said, "Here is a good place to fill up on some more groceries." So Bill jumped off and ran up to the house while I made a big long trip around a big bend in the river. When I got straightened out again, there sat Bill, with a big grin on his face and a big gunny sack full of everything good to eat, even a nice fresh baked cake. That was the life, someone to feed us as we drifted north, of course we paid for all this food as we picked it up, but they didn't charge very much.

We were out about five days when we started to drift through the Vandervert places, Walt Vandervert's ranch was first, then a lot of good water as we neared where "Thousand Trails Camp" is now, but no one lived on the river from Walt Vandervert's place to Bill Vandervert's place. Then we had to go under a foot bridge, it was made real nice and we was a little worried, but we got under real easy and floated on down to the mouth of the Little Deschutes, where we entered the Big Deschutes.

Just before we entered the Big Deschutes, we knew that the brake pole wasn't going to be long enough to reach the bottom of the river, so we stopped and stayed all night before we entered the big river. After supper we went out in the woods and cut two more poles, one about twenty feet long and one about 25 feet long, knowing that we would hit bottom for sure.

Next morning, after a rather hectic sleep — for we were kind of worried about the big river, it sure looked big to us when Swayze pulled the brake on us. Out we went, into the river. When the current hit the lead raft it started to turn crosswise and there wasn't anything we could do about it. Swayze dropped his brake pole to slow us down, but he never, anywhere, touched bottom, even with the long pole. So here we go, the lead raft kept turning until we had a big round ball of lumber right in the middle of the Big Deschutes, and no way to control it. So we just got our bed rolls out and sat down on them, thinking how easy it was going to be from there on to Benham Falls.

But the easy part didn't last very long.

We were all sitting there enjoying the trip and talking about how easy we were making our money, when Bill looked down the river and what do you think he saw about a quarter-mile down river? Harper Bridge was looking right back at him and he said, "My God, look what I see."

We had a big glob of lumber about sixty feet wide and a bridge with two bents out in the river to support the bridge, they were only about sixteen feet apart. Boy did we get up and start to work, but what we didn't know was the lead raft was right about the middle of this raft of lumber.

We began to get a little slack between rafts, but we knew we couldn't last long enough to get them all straight. When I looked down in the bottom of the river and saw some high humps of dirt on the bottom, we all ran back and picked up two of the brake poles and stuck them through the brake hole. Swayze stayed there to hold them while Bill and I tried to get the lead raft out in the lead again. We were about all in when Swayze says, "I have hit something." It was one of the big mounds in the bottom of the river and as luck would have it, the poles held tight. Bill and I got about four of the front rafts about half straightened out when the front raft started under the bridge, so we stayed right there helping the rafts to straighten up, and I think Swayze was praying just a little that his poles would not brake or let go of what he had a hold of.

Well, we got the string all under the bridge and they circled again just like they were on the other side of the bridge. You can guess what we three river rats did, we sat right down on our bed rolls and began to talk about how easy we were earning our money.

We had good going on down to Benham Falls, right up 'til the trucks came along and hauled the lumber on to Bend.

When we got all tied up and our stuff off the rafts and on the bank, we were wonderin' what to do next. Then here comes a big stought Model T Ford and took us back to the saw mill where we started. When we got back to the mill, there was a raft all ready for us to start, so we put our stuff on it and headed out again.

We had better luck with groceries on this trip, we didn't have to bother the ranchers too much, although some of our friends from the trip before came down and had a cup of coffee with us and told us all the news.

Our second trip was lots different from the first one. The company had put on a couple more crews so they helped drag some of the sand bars, and each time we went down it was better.

We had no trouble until we got down to the Vandervert's place, and it seems that some of the other crews would get off on the bank of the river and work from there. I guess they tramped a lot of Vandervert hay down, so they told all of us to stay off their land. We heard about this trouble before we got there so we were going to be real careful. Everything was going real good with us because we could handle the rafts real good by that time, but when we got in sight of their nice new foot bridge, we noticed three of the Vandervert boys standing on the bridge. I was well acquainted with all the boys, so I said to Bill and Swayze, "Let's be damn sure we do things just about right because these boys sure look like they were out for business." As we got close enough to talk, I begun to talk to them, but they weren't very friendly and they informed us that we were to stay on the rafts and not get out on the bank and tramp down any more of their hay. We said we always worked from the rafts, they said be sure you do.

We had the string a straight and ready to go under the bridge, and they went under just like trained sheep. Claude Vandervert was still standing on the bridge when we went under.

Swayze was holding us back real slow and we were doing fine until Bill said to Swayze to turn loose because we had some shallow water to go through. Swayze pulled up his pole and it stuck in the slot and wouldn't pull loose. It hit this nice foot bridge about the middle and here comes the bridge, Claude Vandervert and all, right down on top of our raft. Claude missed the raft and took a high dive right out in the nice clean, cool water. Of course we had most of the foot bridge on top of our raft. About all we could do was to throw the bridge in the river and just keep going. About the last time I saw Claude before he died, he asked me if I remembered the time I gave him a bath in the Little Deschutes River.

From there on we had no trouble to speak of, we even got under the Harper Bridge without any trouble.

That was the last trip I made down the river and we were all happy about that.

The whole deal was a money loosing flunk. I don't really know what become of the mill and those six beautiful horses.

It was a good wet summer and lots of experiences for three river rats.

Most of the time, we could keep the string going, unless we ran into a real bad place, but it was hard work all the time.

No. 16

Oregon in the Pulps

By Bernard A. Drew

Ever hear of Steve Mehan, Arabia Marston or Bearhide Judson? They're figures out of Oregon's past, though you're not likely to read about them in the history books. In fact, the only place you'll find mention of them is in the pages of the pulp fiction magazines of the 1930s and '40s.

For instance: "After a quick meal, a drink and a fresh horse, he mounted and headed out of town for the Oregon border. He rode through Humbug City and Hawkinsville without a stop, and followed a winding trail up the gorge of the Shasta."

Once, after climbing the long slope north of the Klamath, Steve Mehan glimpsed a party of Indians some distance away. "They sighted him, for they turned their horses his way, but he rode on, holding his pace, and crosssed Hungry Creek and left behind him the cairn that marked the boundary line of Oregon. He turned away from the trail then, and headed into the back country, trying a cut-off for Bear Creek and the village of Jacksonville. Somewhere, he lost the Indians." But not for long.

This passage is from Jim Mayo's short story, "Home in the Valley." It originally appeared in the August, 1949, issue of **The Rio Kid Western.** A pulp magazine.

About 30 million readers a month devoured the pulps in their heydays between the world wars. The magazines were printed cheaply, on pulpwood paper, and were bound inside covers depicting breathless action and spine-chilling danger.

As many as 200 titles were on sale at a time, offering an array of yarns about cowboys, ape men and air aces, hard-boiled detectives, space rangers and bug-eyed creatures, beautiful women and ugly villains and virile super heroes.

Among the latter were The Shadow and Doc Savage, Secret Agent X and Nick Carter and a host of others.

Pulp magazine readers had an insatiable thirst for new faces, new scenery. Writers, working at a frantic pace for only a penny or two a word, accommodated them with excursions to every corner of the globe. Oregon was a handy setting for dozens of

speeding chases, bold confrontations and blazing gun battles — such as the one between Steve Mehand and the Indians.

Because of a bank failure, Mehan's cattle drive is doomed to financial failure. Unless he can get to the Oregon branch office before the news arrives. His cross-country race is against time, a San Francisco steamboat, and marauding Indians.

". . . Wild yells chorused behind him, and a shot cut the branches overhead. He fired again, and then again.

"Stowing the Smith and Wesson away, he whipped out the four-barrel Braendlin. Holding it ready, he charged out of the brush and headed across the open country. Behind him the Modocs were coming fast. His horse was quick and alert, and he swung it around a grove of trees and down into a gully. Racing along the bottom, he hit a small stream and began walking the horse carefully upstream. After making a half mile, he rode out again and took to the timber . . ."

One hundred and forty-three hours after leaving San Francisco, Mehan completes his journey.

Not all Beaver State pulp characters are honorable or heroic. Particularly those from Portland. Arabia Marston is the pretty criminal who fends off Secret Service agent Kelly in Victor Maxwell's tale "Why Arabia Kissed Me" (**The Popular Magazine** August 20, 1916).

A notorious smuggler in Portland and up and down the Pacific Coast, Arabia is in serious trouble. She convinces Kelly's friend Smith, who has fallen in love with her, to help her trick the government agent and avoid arrest. The kiss is his reward.

Grizzley Oregon mountain man Judson has troubles of another sort in Roy M. O'Mara's 1944 yarn, "Bearhide's Moonshine War": "Officer Perry Fletcher assumed his favorite stance, with feet spread and knotted fists jammed against his hips. 'Look,' he snapped, 'that elk is property of the state. You touch one hair on his hide and I'll have you back in the jailhouse — where you belong

anyway.'

"Cold fear was clutching the vitals of Bearhide Judson, but not from the tirades of the blustering game warden. Bearhide's eyes were fastened on a huge, bald headed man, bellied up to the table inside the house, stowing away great fragments of meat that looked and smelled like venison. It was 'Mash' Merritt, the revenue man, known and feared by every illegal still operator from Phoenix to Seattle.

" 'Yes, sir!' Bearhide mumbled, and backed away."

The pulps had a reputation for printing stories containing stock situations, one-dimensional characters, and plain hack writing. But they were good!

Through the years, they nurtured a number of writers who went on to success in the slick magazine and hardcover book markets. Among these were John D. MacDonald and Tennessee Williams, Ray Bradbury, Erle Stanley Gardner, Edgar Rice Burroughs and Ernest Haycox.

Not all of the pulp fictioneers who employed the off-trail Oregon setting benefited from the first-hand knowledge of writers such as Haycox, who was born in the state. Most of them faked it. "A man didn't have to do a lot of research," commented pulp penman Richard Wilkinson. "Neither the editors nor the readers worried much about accuracy as to facts, locations, or periods in which the story happened. If it was good entertainment, that's all that mattered."

Well, the pulps certainly could be entertaining.

Consider the adventures of young forester Zip Sawyer, who is shot at while sky topping a big Douglas fir, in Vance Richardson's "Sky Topping with Death" (**Top-Notch** January 1933).

Sawyer finds himself caught up in a feud between the Ilqua River Lumber Company and a homesteader named Gorriby. At stake is a sky line which would carry logs over Gorriby's land to the railhead.

The pulp writer couldn't resist

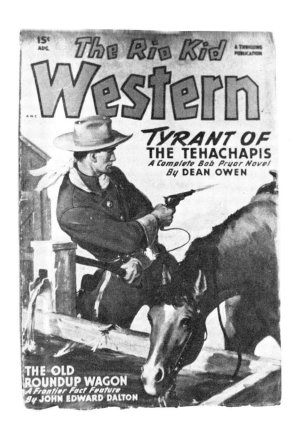

taking a stab a Oregonians: " ' Why do the Gorribys object to the sky line?' asked Zip. 'Not a log would touch their land unless the rigging gave way.'

" 'Why do some of these old webfoot Oregon mossbacks object to anything?' growled the foreman. 'Just general cussedness, I guess...' "

Perhaps to make up for such affronts, the pulp mag editors from time to time inserted obscure tidbits of Oregon lore. For example, one 1952 issue of **The Rio Kid Western** related the mishaps of Widow Marcey, who took two years to travel from Kentucky to Northern Oregon.

"When the Widow Marcey reached)regon it was obvious that she ouldn't very well take up land and arm it by herself. But what of the dozens of men who had no wives and were farming? They were cooking and mending for themselves, but not too well. Mrs. Marcey made arrangements with them. For a fixed sum she visited their 'homes' twice each week, during which period she prepared in advance an adequate and suitable amount of food, mended their clothes and cleaned the place up properly.

"Apparently the men liked the idea, for soon Mrs. Marcey had more clients than she could handle and engaged another woman to help her."

The fiction writers ultimately recognized Oregon as a strong shaper of character, both human and animal, as we see in these next two stories.

"Barrel 'Em and Bend 'Em" by T.R. Ellis, from the February 15, 1932, issue of **Adventure**, is a car racing story.

"On the second day of July, several years back," we are told, "I'm sittin' in a hotel lobby up in Midtown, Oregon. I'm readin' over an entry blank, which I already know by heart, wherein the management of the Midtown Speedway informs me that the annual 100-mile Speed Classic is to be held two days hence. All of which is like rubbin' salt in a cut, because I got a perfectly good Miller Special, with plenty of revolutions under the bonnet, all tuned up and nobody to drive it. Leo Heisman has been performin' that service for me, until one of his relations died and left him so much money that he is henceforth and forever ruined as a race driver."

The promoter hires a down-and-outer named Smitty, who wins the race — and turns out to be a top European driver who lost his nerve following a crackup. This was the only way he could prove himself

again.

In Vingie E. Roe's "A Thoroughbred" (**The Popular Magazine** February 7, 1917), a Frenchman named Gaston buys an ill-marked, seemingly vicious Airedale named Grip. Some instinct tells Gaston that the dog has "a heart above all fear," and he takes it with him to the north timber country of Oregon to prove it.

"For days they climbed into the dripping dust of the Coast Range, among the towering pines, firs and spruces.

"They stopped for nights in this thicket or under that jutting rock, and Gaston made great, roaring fires from the abundance of resinous woods that choked the underway."

The dog Grip soon shows his worth by protecting a young boy from three coyotes: "He knew that he was to fight, and fight hard, and all his big-boned body was aching for the fray, but he trembled with fear lest, in the fracas, and enemy snatch at the boy."

Oregon residents enjoyed the pulps immensely. Many joined the Doc Savage Club or the Friends of the Phantom. Others wrote letters to the magazine editors praising stories or grumbling about ones they didn't like.

This letter from Pvt. Al Wright, Pendleton Field, Pendleton, Oregon, was printed in the Summer, 1943 issue of **Captain Future**, a science fiction magazine. "I had to write and tell you what I think of **Captain Future**. I think it is the best mag of its kind on the market. I can't complain about it because I read it from cover to cover. I believe I have read every issue since it came out . . . "

The pulps didn't last much beyond the 1940s. Television entertainment and paperback novels combined with wartime paper shortages to kill them.

During their lifetime, the pulps had a wide and varied readership. " . . . Harry S. Truman and Al Capone were each on the subscription list at Popular at about the same time," claimed Henry Steeger, a pulp magazine publisher. "Truman subscribed to one of the Detective magazines and Capone subscribed to one of the Western books, although you might have thought it would have been the other way around."

Today a whole new generation of readers is delighting in the paperback reprintings of the original, outrageous pulps — the great adventures of Doc Savage and The Shadow, Philip Marlowe and Jim Hatfield and Conan of Cimmeria.

You may not find their names in the history books, but Steve Mehan, Arabia Marston and the like played a role in Oregon's rich heritage.

During their lifetime, the pulps had a wide and varied readership. "... Harry S. Truman and Al Capone were each on the subscription list at Poplar at about the same time ..."

If you enjoyed Volume I...you're sure to enjoy

Little Known Tales from Oregon History

Volume II

See page 87 for information about Little Known Tales, Volume III

Silver Lake Cemetery Monument listing names of 43 fire victims.
Oregon Historical Society Photo

Silver Lake Christmas Tragedy

By Richard H. Syring
Reprinted from Northwest Magazine

Mrs. Vera Poorman of Salem.
Believed to be the last survivor alive
Richard H. Syring Photo   of the Silver Lake Fire.

Smoke alarms and chemical fire extinguishers were unknown in 1894. Even if they had been, probably there would have been little chance that they would have done any good in the remote community of Silver Lake. In Silver Lake, in 1894, it was "The Night Before Christmas." Creatures were stirring, but there were no reindeer happily dashing over snow-covered roofs. Instead, only steeds of death — horrible fiery death — were to stalk that little community on that Christmas Eve.

After nearly 85 years, the tragedy remains unforgettably seared in Oregon's history as the worst destruction of life by fire ever. Forty-three men, women and children died as a result of the fire.

At the time, Silver Lake was a prosperous livestock and wood-producing area. In 1894, Silver Lake was only six years old and the only established trading post between Prineville and Lakeview. It had been homesteaded mainly by settlers from

SISTERS REDMOND
20 126 PRINEVILLE
BEND
97 20
LA PINE
31
SILVER LAKE
OREGON

Lane County.

This community of 150 souls was on the stagecoach route in 1894, and mail arrived twice weekly. The nearest railroad was 200 miles away. The community gathering place was the Chrisman Brothers General Store. Upstairs was what was called the J.W. Clayton Hall, where dances often were held weekly over a pine board floor. It also was used for dinners and other special occasions.

What passed for a hotel was located across a dirt road from Chrisman's store. There was a hitching rack where cowboys and ranch hands tied up their horses before going into the hostelry for a drink. There probably were fewer than 35 buildings in Silver Lake, and, like most central Oregon communities, it was unincorporated; hence it had no voluntary fire department.

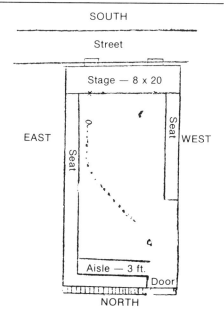

Oregon Historical Society Drawings

CHRISMAN & Co.'s Store at Silver Lake

SOUTH
Street
Stage — 8 x 20
Seat
EAST   Seat   Seat   WEST
Aisle — 3 ft.
Door
NORTH

But there was a medical doctor and a lot of good people. These were the kind of people, due to the remoteness of the area, who liked every opportunity to gather in the hall above the Chrisman Brothers store.

Dec. 24, 1894, dawned cold and clear. There was some snow on the ground. Well before noon, freight outfits began pulling up in front of the store, with six- or eight-horse teams and their drivers riding high-wheelers, jerk lines in hand. Wagons and smaller buggies kept discharging the warmly bundled adults and children.

Upstairs all day, a committee of women prepared for the traditional Christmas Eve celebration. Festoons of fragrant pine decorated the bare-walled monotony of the hall, which was about 20 feet wide and 50 feet deep, with an eight-foot-deep stage. The stage was on the opposite end of the hall from the door leading to the stairway.

A large coal oil (kerosene) lamp stood on the organ by the stage. Several Rochester lamps, each holding more than a gallon of oil, hung from the low ceiling. It was to be a festive occasion for some 170 men, women and children, many of whom had traveled many miles to get there.

By the time dinner was over and benches of boards had been arranged in rows, anticipation was mounting. Some little girls were dressed as angels. And, of course, there were the "Three Wise Men." None of the early accounts of the time describes a Santa Claus. And little did anyone dream of the horrible fate to be met shortly.

Once the Christmas Eve exercises were over, restless persons jockeyed for better viewing positions where they could see the stage and gift presentation better. One was George Payne, 18, who started walking on top of a bench from the rear of the hall. He either wanted a better view or was headed for the doorway at the head of the stairs.

Payne's head struck a Rochester lamp. He tried to right it and spilled some of the flammable oil. The lamp blazed. Spilled oil was on the dry pine board floor.

The blazing lamp caused panic, eventually leading to death by fire or trampling of 19 women, 16 men and eight children — 43 in all. Those not killed that night died several days later. Scores were badly burned or injured.

Had cool heads prevailed, there might have been no loss of life. Oregon's historical fire tragedy might not have taken place. Francis M. Chrisman, one of the brothers who owned the building, grabbed the lamp out of the chandelier and started for the door. The blazing lamp increased the panic, and it was knocked from his hands. It dropped to the floor and many persons started kicking it toward the door — only to spread the flames.

As panic mounted, some tried to beat out the flames with their coats. But it was hardly two minutes after the lamp fell (another was knocked to the floor from the organ) that the whole building was aflame. Unfortunately at first, there were cries of "Close the door! It can be put out!" This, probably at first, prevented more people from escaping.

Fear took over. Some knelt in prayer. Everyone screamed orders, but none obeyed. Calm men of good will a few minutes before became panic-stricken. The rush to the narrow door leading to the stairway was so great that many were knocked to the floor and trampled to death.

Some years after the fire, Augustus Schroeder remembered that he was shoved against the door, forced into the hallway and toppled over the bannister by the weight of the pressing throng. He got outside with few injuries, but his wife and son perished.

What made matters worse, people on the outside heroically dashed up the narrow stairway, trying to rescue persons inside. This only clogged the passageway worse. Turmoil reigned.

Meanwhile, one of the cooler heads, Warren Duncan, who a few minutes earlier had been one of "The Three Wise Men," raced to the opposite end of the room and kicked out a window leading to a small balcony over the store's entrance.

"Everyone out this way," Duncan shouted, striving to be heard over the dreadful roar of the flames.

Many rushed to this new avenue of escape. Duncan assisted women and children through the broken glass. Soon the balcony was overcrowded.

Suddenly, the overweighted balcony collapsed, pitching sobbing, shuddering men, women and children 15 feet to the ground. Many, fortunate to escape the flames, were killed or seriously injured. However, a ladder placed against the window sill allowed others to escape.

Meanwhile, attempts to throw water up the stairway with a hand pump were futile. The water did, however, help douse the fire on persons who stumbled out with clothing ablaze.

After the last person was rescued, not one cry or moan could be heard over the crackly roar of the fire, it was reported later. Those still inside had suffocated or were cremated.

Among those saved was 7-month-old Veva Buick, carried out in the arms of her father, John Buick, who had his 8-year-old son, Frank, by the hand. Buick's wife and two other children perished.

Veva Buick, later Veva Poorman, a sprightly, alert widow who turned 85 last May and a resident of a Lutheran home in Salem's Keizer district, recalled the horror stories told by her father and other survivors.

"When everything was burned, they started looking for me," she said, adding with a grin, "They found me on the bar of the saloon across the street. Father apparently thought that was a safe place for me when he went back to search for other members of our family."

Every household in Silver Lake was touched by the tragedy. Fifteen members of the Owsley family, including in-laws, were lost in the blaze. Every house became a hospital or first-aid station. In one was George Payne, who reportedly accidentally started the fire. He died several days later.

Silver Lake's only doctor was many miles away for the holidays at the time of the fire. A young man by the name of Ed O'Farrell galloped on horesback for the only medic available — Dr. Bernard Daly at Lakeview — about 100 miles away. He had to change mounts four times. The pair arrived several days later.

In 1894, Silver Lake was so remote that news of the holocaust did not reach the outside world for two or three days.

"Frightful Holocaust" was the headline on one newspaper story. Another read, "A Silver Lake Horror."

Portland businessmen and citizens generously responded to the need for financial help. They sent $300 to pay for medicines and nursing during the remainder of the winter.

Despite their tragedy, citizens of Silver Lake sent word back to Portland on Jan. 29, 1895, that they had had enough charity and could get along.

Today, as you drive through Silver Lake on Oregon 31, headed south toward Lakeview, there remains a grim reminder of the tragic fire. On the left, just outside town, there is an imposing marble monument nearly 10 feet tall. It dwarfs the smaller headstones in the cemetery.

No. 18

During the course of building Oregon, many dramatic, important events took place and are so recorded in our history books. At the same time, many little, unimportant events took place, which should also be remembered, not for being historically significant, but as an indication of man's continuous struggle against weather, fate and misfortune. Such is the case of bringing the first electric power plant to Burns and told here for the first time in print.

Today, as we pass the big electric generating plants throughout Oregon, it's difficult to visualize that some of our cities have obtained electric power only since the turn of the century. For example, Burns did not have electricity until June 1902, and then only after some extensive campaigning by local residents and, subsequently, a rather harrowing period of battling the weather to get the machinery delivered and installed.

On January 19, 1901, the Burns Times-Herald carried a scorching editorial, stating, "The people of Burns would like to have electric lights and water works." As result of this and other efforts, a Mr. M.V. Gates of Hillsboro visited Burns, during May of 1901, to analyze the needs and potential of the town, and to talk with city officials about installing an electric plant and water system. He advised it would take $30,000 to put in a suitable plant.

During the months which followed, city officials received proposals by several individuals and finally, on January 25, 1902, F.N. Averill and the City of Burns reached an agreement, providing for Mr. Averill to install an electric generator, to be in operation within 6 months. Power for the generator was to be furnished by Joe Sturdevant's grist mill, one mile north of Burns. On June 21, 1902, the Times-Herald proudly reported "The electric lights, which were turned on for the first time this week, brightened things up wonderfully. They are giving good satisfaction."

However, this was a prematurely optimistic observation, for the problems of the young electric company were only beginning. During the following weeks the company was plagued with one headache after another. The plant would break down, overloaded lines caused troubles, there were great fluctuations in the power-output resulting in flickering of the lights, people bitterly complained about not being able to depend upon the power. Customers also complained about the excessive rate of "$1.25 per month for the first light and 50¢ for each additional light of no more than 16 candlepower" . . . comparable to, but providing considerably less illumination than a present day 20-watt bulb.

Mr. Averill finally became disgusted with the whole thing and sold control to The Electric Light & Power Co. which was incorporated during August for the purpose of buying the struggling company. H.M. Horton was elected president of the new company; C. Cummins, vice-president; N.U. Carpenter, treasure; and F. O. Jackson, secretary. Early in September they assumed management of the company and immediately announced that a new, larger dynamo had been ordered, with a powerful 60 horsepower engine and a new boiler. Big plans were under way. But their problems had just begun.

Equipment of this type had to be ordered from the east, shipped by railroad to Huntington, where it would be transferred to freight wagons, hopefully arriving in Burns

When Electricity Came to Burns

By Art Chipman

a week or two, or more, later, depending upon the weather and condition of the dirt roads.

During November, the company was notified the equipment had arrived in Huntington and arrangements were made with "Jap" McKinnon and his brother to haul it to Burns. But the weather turned bad. It began to snow. Nights were freezing cold. Mr. McKinnon and his brother finally reached Huntington, loaded most of the equipment on their wagons and started back to Burns. It continued to snow. During the day the road was a quagmire. At night the cold turned them numb. After several days they unloaded part of the machinery and tried to make it with the balance. A few days later, almost exhausted, they reached the Kate Fopian ranch at the foot of Bendier Mountain, between West Fall & Beulah. And, while it had temporarily stopped snowing, the weather was still bitterly cold. The two brothers decided to give up the whole miserable project and forget all the time and effort invested. Unloading the boiler at the ranch, the weary men returned to Burns where they advised the company management that the equipment could not be brought through until the next year when the roads were better. At this time (early December 1902) Mr. Horton was inter-

Sam Gould, freighter and rancher in early day Harney County.

BELOW: Sam Gould's jerk-line team and freight wagon on the 1901 highway from Huntington to Burns.

viewed by the local newspaper as to the progress of the new plant and he disgustedly exclaimed, "The company now has machinery scattered all over eastern Oregon with not a whole piece in Burns."

After frantic discussions as to what could be done with the machinery strewn along the road from Huntington, they called on Samuel W. Gould, a well known freighter, who lived in nearby Harney City. They urged him to try and get the equipment to Burns before winter closed in completely. Mr. Gould agreed to see if it could be brought in. Early the next morning he and his wife, Emma, started out on horseback to examine the various pieces of machinery and to ascertain what would be needed to get it loaded and delivered. Upon his return, several days later, Mr. Gould advised them it would be a very difficult project but he felt he could accomplish the job if the weather didn't turn worse and he was willing to try.

Sam Gould rented a couple of additional horses to add to his 8 horse team, hired a 6 horse team and wagon with Charlie Crawford to drive it, and left to bring back the equipment. The weather did not worsen, although it didn't improve any either, with incessant shifting snow and freezing nights. The more than hundred mile

The modern power plant which serves Burns today is a far cry from the primitive little operation of 1903, but it took tough men and a tough little lady, too, to get that first plant there so those 16 candlepower light bulbs could keep shining bright and regular.

drive was extremely uncomfortable. Hurriedly, the men loaded most of the vital equipment, including the huge boiler and started back to Burns. Sam Gould drove the 10 horse jerk-line team, straining to pull the heavier load through the mud, and Crawford followed with the lighter outfit. Only a few tiring miles could be covered each day. Frequently they would become stuck in deep mud holes whereupon Sam Gould would climb on Tige, his big, brown wheel horse, to yell loud encouragement at the team, urging them on. At times like these, Mrs. Gould would climb off the wagon and trot alongside the team, calling at them to pull harder, sometimes she would throw small rocks at the horses to get them to give a greater effort.

After a number of days and a great deal of difficulty, they struggled to the top of Stinking Water Pass, some 40 or 50 miles east of Burns. Upon starting down the mountain, the two new horses became excited and caused the whole team to run away. Down the mountain they dashed, their hame-bells jangling, the wagon bumping along the rocky road, Mr. Gould desperately guided them with the long jerk-line, trying to bring them under control. Miraculously, he guided them down without wrecking the wagon or spilling the load and finally his familiar voice brought his regular eight horses under control. Charlie Crawford brought the second and lighter load down without difficulty.

It was continuing to snow lightly and the 2 teams were having an increasingly harder time. Each day the horses and the men were just a little more exhausted. Mr. Gould was utilizing every freighter trick he knew to keep the wagons moving without over-taxing the horses. Stops would be made on the top of rises, to give a down hill start for the horses and he would carefully examine the road ahead to avoid all obsticals possible. He loved his horses and would have left the equipment rather than injure them but he had worked with his team for years and knew their capacity. However, he had a job which he had promised to accomplish if at all possible, and he aimed to do just that.

It was so cold that clouds of steam arose from the sweaty horses and every breath by man and beast was a white spout of steam. Nights were pure misery, with quick meals being cooked by the intrepid young Mrs. Gould over a struggling campfire, often with blowing snow to add further discomfort. At night they had

to go to bed to keep warm and in the mornings everything would be frozen, making it a real chore to fix a breakfast.

Christmas came, and was spent on the road, still a few miles from Burns. They couldn't gamble the time to go home for Christmas. The young children staying with Mrs. Gould's family would help them celebrate later.

On December 26, 1902, the 2 big wagons, loaded with machinery and the huge, new boiler, rolled into Burns, down the snow and ice covered streets to the site of the power plant. The hame-bells triumphantly jingled in the crisp, frosty air and excited youngsters ran alongside yelling. They had been almost 3 weeks on the trail with most of the nights spent in the wagons, for ranches were few and far between along the road.

After a day's rest and a belated Christmas, Mr. and Mrs. Gould, along with Charlie Crawford, returned for the balance of the machinery. The weather was still extremely cold, with a light snow falling to bother them. The remaining equipment was quickly loaded on the wagons and by mid-January they were back in Burns where the grateful power company officials put it to good use in providing dependable electricity for the first time. A day or so later, the winter storms broke with full fury; had they delayed any further it would have been months before the equipment could have reached the town.

The modern power plant which serves Burns today is a far cry from the primitive little operation of 1903, but it took tough men and a tough little lady, too, to get that first plant there so those 16 candlepower light bulbs could keep shining bright and regular. Not a story of great heroism, just a little forgotten episode of sturdy people rising to the occasion, giving the "maximum effort" in helping to build our state, and who should not be forgotten.

The Chinese Mail Service

By Robert Joe Stout

An old Western legend describes the immigrant Chinaman's first encounter with the rugged U.S. mail service: the envelope addressed to San Francisco was squeezed, torn open, shaken over a scales; its yield of an ounce or two of gold dust promptly pocketed and the Chinaman flung against a post and beaten, his queue burned to the top of his head and his clothes searched for more gold. Later, accused of thievery, he was tried and hanged.

And his first encounter with West Coast innkeepers: able to pay his night's lodging with a measureable portion of dust, he was shown to a room and as soon as he fell asleep, was raided, tortured and robbed. Penniless, without defense and almost naked, he was thrown into a sub-freezing cold and had he not been young enough to jog twenty miles to the nearest Chinese settlement, he would have died of frostbite.

By 1851, two-and-a-half years after the discovery of gold near Coloma, California, there already were an estimated 15,000 Chinese in California, Oregon and Nevada. Like the Australians, Chileans and Americans who'd poured into the land of gold, they were the descendants of poor farmers and shopkeepers whose future in their homeland was a web of poverty, oppression and imprisonment. Unlike the Europeans and Americans, however, they banded together, despite disparate Oriental backgrounds (China at the time was a clustered network of Feudal satraphies and overlordships comprising several hundred separate dialects and social arrangements). They carefully mined the tailings left behind by more impatient Anglos, formed communal ventures and concealed their few big finds in order to send money to their relatives in the old land.

Unlike either the Mexicans or Indians, who separately and individually had governed most of the West in carefree, nomadic fashion and actively resented the intruder whites, the Chinese recognized their own subsidiary position and worked around it. San Francisco, then Portland, became centers of Chinese initiative. Because laundries and restaurants required the least capital, those two businesses multiplied under Chinese management.

Thousands of other Chinese laid rails, dug dams and built rock fences all the way from British Columbia to Mexico, west to the Pacific and east to Wyoming and Montana. Because they could not trust either the infant postal service nor the provincial Anglo banking establishments, they developed a banking and communications system of their own.

Dave Cheng, himself an old man when I talked to him in his elaborately maintained San Francisco home, repeated stories he had heard about the first of his family to come to America. The older Cheng had been one of an elite group of couriers who had transported their countrymen's earnings from outlying places like Roseburg, Oregon, Fallon, Nevada and Pocatello, Idaho, to the Chinese enterprises in Portland and San Francisco.

In return, he brought them certain essential supplies: dried squid, joss sticks, dried vegetables, tea, icons and opium.

"He was very cautious," Dave explained, "and never wore good clothing or let on in any way that he was carrying thousands of dollars concealed amoung his rags." Whenever possible, he traveled with Chinese companions, since a lone Oriental in a remote part of the gold country was in danger of harassment, if not torture and death. Instead of buying food, or paying for boat or stagecoach passage, he would hire himself out as a stable-sweep or dishwasher, deckhand or woodcutter, in exchange for food and passage. He followed a more or less definite series of stops, delivering little items precious to the immigrants and giving them both letters and the latest rumors and news. The Chinese shopkeepers, miners and laborers paid him either in money or with food, lodging and portions of their imports and entrusted him with savings they wanted their relatives in the Old World to receive.

They also gave him messages to deliver for friends, both along his route and in Portland and San Francisco. More often than not, the news was bad. The high birthrate among the Chinese living in more populated centers was complemented by an even higher deathrate and the shifting pogroms and work projects drove or lured many Chinese into far-flug parts of the country. One detour into the thinly populated goldcamps in northeastern Jackson County brought Cheng to swept-clean remains that once had been a line of jerry-built Chinese cabins. The only evidence that Chinese once had lived there was the carved cariacature of a pig-tailed face on an exposed slab of sandstone behind it. When Cheng moved closer to examine it, he found half-a-dozen columns of figures. The miners, the message in Chinese script reported, has run into difficulties in the camp and had decided to move to Fort Klamath for the winter. There Cheng delivered the news, tea and dried delicacies that otherwise never would have reached them.

On another trip Cheng came upon what he thought was an abandoned wagon with a broken axle. Thinking he could spend the night in it, he pulled back the flap — and was greeted by a scream! Huddled among robes and blankets was a nearly starved and hysterical white woman with a two-week-old baby. From supplies that he was carrying, Cheng brewed an Oriental remedy, which he induced both the woman and the child to take. The woman's husband had taken their two horses and gone for help, leaving her in the wagon over a week. Cheng guided her and the baby into the nearest town, where she was taken in by the stabler's family until her husband could be found.

Cheng wisely left town before he could be accused of playing a part in the man's disappearance. Through other contacts he was told that the woman regained her health and took her child back to Tennessee, where her parents lived. The man never was found: Cheng believed he had gotten lost or injured and his horses fallen prey to mountain lions in the rugged country he was trying to cross. He also was told that the woman had praised him for saving her life and had argued his cause against suggestions that he'd been involved in her husband's murder.

No all of Cheng's clients were men. The Feudal Chinese culture of the mid-19th century did not elevate women's rights and it was not uncommon for chinese parents to sell their daughters into prostitution. One young girl, barely thirteen, saved her meager earnings from a frontier bawdyhouse and had Cheng send them to her father. "So different from what children feel now," the younger Cheng shook his head. "And from what parents do, thankfully," he added with a wry, inturned smile.

As far as the son could tell, the elder Cheng had not followed any specific timetable. However, most of his courier journeys began and ended in San Francisco and Portland. Apparently he often went from the California city to Eureka, on the coast, by packet, crossed the mountains to Weaverville, which had a large Chinese community, and worked his way north through Ashland into Jacksonville, Gold Hill and Roseburg. From there, he proceeded northward to Portland and, sometimes, Seattle. Then, depending upon how much wealth and "mail" he was carrying (either personally or in his head) he would return to San Francisco by boat or take the inland route along the Cascades.

"I think he was never robbed," Dave Cheng nodded. "Or if he was, he never told me of it." He was, however, harassed, and often slept in alleyways and stables when he could not find a Chinese family to take him in. He sometimes hid the gold he carried in a piece of cabbage or turnip and more than once returned to the city carrying the ashes of an immigrant whose dying request had been that he be buried in China with his ancestors.

The informal "Chinese mail service," of which the elder Cheng was a part, continued into this century. By then, enough Chinese had attained positions of respect and authority to guarantee their equality as far as mail, travel and communications were concerned. How many of the couriers, like Cheng, developed solid merchantile businesses isn't known, but the figure is probably quite high. They were, for many years, the only contact that the often persecuted Chinese miners and laborers had with their heritage and their respect and appreciation of those who carried their messages (and their wealth) must have been quite high.

Teanamad: He Once Ruled Central Oregon!

By David Braly

There was a time when a town in Baker County was the largest city in the Northwest. Auburn was the town and it was at the center of the eastern Oregon gold rush of the early 1860s. A few miles further west, Canyon City in Grant County was the second largest town in the region. Portland trailed at third in population.

Prospectors seeking gold, merchants after quick dollars, and cattlemen attracted by rich grazing lands had populated eastern Oregon quickly. Although the big attractions were the gold fields of Baker and Grant counties, stockmen had already moved into the valleys of Grande Ronde, Ochoco and Harney. Log cabins, plank stage stations, and herds of cattle and horses had begun to appear everywhere in the region.

There were only two impediments to settlement, beside, of course, the rough terrain and harsh climatic changes of the Oregon outback. One was the outlaws, often organized into large gangs, who frontier law seldom touched. Gangs like Plummer's Rustlers could and did get away with cold-blooded murder in the mining regions. The second impediment was the Paiutes (also called Shoshonis and Snakes), who attacked lonely travelers, pack trains, wagons, and even settlements.

Oregon's Superintendent of Indian Affairs, J.W.P. Huntington, was anxious to end the Paiute troubles in the eastern region of the state. He called the chiefs of all Indian tribes together for a peace parley at Fort Klamath in 1864.

One chief ignored the summons. This was the leader of the Walpapi Paiutes, Teanamad. Of all the Paiute chiefs in the outback, Teanamad was regarded as being most responsible for white deaths. There had been several attempts to bring him under thumb. On May 18, 1863, a cavalry company seeking him in the Crooked River country had fallen into an ambush on Maury Creek and suffered heavy casualties. Teanamad's failure to appear at Fort Klamath meant that Huntington's plans to settle everything were ruined and the superintendent was angry.

After the conference ended, the Huntington party began the long journey back to The Dalles. While following the Deschutes, they came upon an Indian encampment. Huntington's men quickly killed the three men in the camp and took the three women and two children prisoner. It turned out that Huntington had captured the family of Teanamad himself. They were taken as hostages back to Fort Klamath. When he heard the news, Teanamad rode to the fort, and, on August 12, 1865, agreed to live in peace on the Klamath Indian Reservation.

Unfortunately, the food that the government had promised Teanamad's people was not forthcoming. They became hungry and slipped off the reservation. Teanamad, however, stayed, and waited for the food. Autumn turned to winter and winter to spring, but still there was no food. At last, Teanamad left the reservation and joined his people at Summer Lake. He bought guns from other chiefs and prepared to drive the white people out of central Oregon.

Chief Teanamad, struck with such brutality, the reasons for his war were eclipsed by its horrors. He set up headquarters in the Upper Beaver Creek Valley and Paulina Valley of southern Crook County. From there, he struck across central Oregon, stealing cattle and horses, burning houses and driving out almost every white

settler between the Cascades and the Blue Mountains. The human heads which gave Skull Hollow its name were among his victims.

The army sent the First U.S. Cavalry in a 630-mile sweep across the outback in an attempt to snare Teanamad. The cavalry destroyed several Indian villages and won two pitched battles, but not with Teanamad, who was busy slaughtering peaceful Modocs in the Sprague River valley.

In August, scores of Indians raided the Elk and Dixie creek areas near Canyon City, killing, burning, and stealing. Teanamad made the road between The Dalles and Canyon City a trail of death. Central Oregon was completely abandoned by its few settlers and was the exclusive domain of Teanamad's Paiutes. Further east, transportation and communication ended, schools closed, and business came to a standstill. The previously booming economy of Canyon City slid into a depression. Prices went out of sight because supplies seldom got through. Even the army was on the defensive. Teanamad defeated the soldiers repeatedly and his brother, Chief Wahveveh, threw his warriors against Camp Wright and burned it to the ground.

Only occasionally did Teanamad lose, even though he was fighting the Klamaths, Modocs, and Warm Springs Indians as well as the whites. Billy Chinook, the famous Warm Springs scout, beat some of his warriors. The Warm Springs Indian hated Teanamad because he constantly raided their reservation and had treacherously murdered two of their chiefs, Queapama and Poustaminie. In the summer of 1866, Chinook and 25 of his warriors surprised a Paiute camp on Dry Creek, 13 miles from modern Prine-

ville, and killed or captured 32 hostiles after a fierce battle in the forest. Another setback for the chief came at Steen Mountain above Lake Harney. The army found him there (it was one of his favorite hunting spots) and he had to take refuge in a cave. Although the Paiute warriors drove back and defeated the soldiers, Wahveveh was killed in the battle.

All through the winter of 1866-67, Teanamad killed and plundered. Central Oregon was now his. All that remained of the white man between The Dalles and Canyon City was a few stage stations. The ranchers who had begun to move into the Deschutes and Crooked River valleys had left. They would not return until this enemy was dead.

They did not have to wait long. On April 25, 1867, the chief's band stole 25 head of cattle and horses from Andrew Clarno's stage station. They were spotted by James Clark, whose own station's encounter with Teanamad earned it the name "Burnt Ranch." Clark fetched another station owner, Howard Maupin, who had earlier lost horses to Teanamad's raiders. They and two other men quietly pursued the Paiutes to a camp on Trout Creek (Jefferson Co.).

They eluded the lookouts, dismounted in a secluded location, and crawled as close to camp as they dared. Then they opened fire with their rifles. The Indians fled into the nearby hills, except for one tall Paiute dressed in an old blue cavalry coat, wounded in the thigh by Maupin. Clark recognized the wounded Indian as one who had tried to kill him during a long chase the previous September, asked Maupin for permission to finish him, and, upon receiving it, shot him three times.

After a search of the area failed to turn up any more Indians, the group looted the camp, scalped the dead Indian, and rounded up Clarno's stock. Only later did they learn that the Indian they had slain was Teanamad.

The body rotted where it fell. White men had always called the chief "Paulina" or "Paunina" instead of Teanamad, and the place where he fell is now known as Paulina Basin. Wherever he had been, people in Central Oregon remembered. His old headquarters is now the town of Paulina. But today, oddly, few people know how that one Indian left his name on so much of Oregon geography. Central Oregon history is usually started at 1868, the year Prineville was founded, and it is frequently forgotten that there were settlers in the region much earlier who were driven out by Teanamad. The settlers themselves, never forgot.

Of all the Paiute chiefs in the outback, Teanamand was regarded as being most responsible for white deaths. There had been several attempts to bring him under thumb.

No. 21
Klondike Kate in Central Oregon

Text & Photos by Ellis Lucia

On a certain day back in 1914, a group of teamsters hauling supplies to Millican paused for supper at Dunn's Place some eight miles out of Bend. Suddenly there was a great commotion in the yard. The diners flung open the door on a memorable scene.

A cursing driver was trying to hang onto a jittery horse with one hand and calm a raging redhead in a big plume hat, glittering dancehall gown, flashing jewelry and red dancing slippers with the other. She was wailing something about that crazy horse which threw her into the dust, spraining her ankle.

The boys helped her inside where Mrs. Dunn popped her into bed, limping and groaning every step of the way. Yet soon after being fed, she called out to the boys: "Would one of you nice fellows come in here and hold my head? I feel so sick . . ." And a bit later she tempted them with her bottle. But among the teamsters were no takers, for if their womenfolk heard about it, there'd be the devil to pay.

That was Klondike Kate's debut to central Oregon, and from that moment for the remainder of her long and colorful life, she was on stage most all the time. Central Oregon, Prineville and Bend, although still close to the wild frontier, didn't always approve of the Queen of the Yukon, but people never forgot her, for she cloaked herself in mystery. She became one of Bend's most celebrated citizens, central Oregon's first rockhound, and today ranks among Oregon's most legendary characters of the Old West.

Klondike Kate Rockwell, native of Kansas via Spokane and the Frozen North, fell in love with the region east of the Cascades during a horseback trip while Hill and Harriman were battling over the railroad in the Deschutes River canyon. Many former Yukoners were taking up homesteads on the High Desert. Kate returned to Seattle, trying to rebuild her life from a broken love affair with Alexander Pantages, her live-in boyfriend of Dawson days. Later, in Seattle and Vancouver, British Columbia, Pantages and Kate launched what would become one of the nation's greatest vaudeville theater chains, using Kate's Yukon grubstake. When he married another entertainer, Kate sued for "breach of promise," settling after gaudy headlines for "something less than five thousand dollars." But Pantages was never completely rid of her.

After scandal and heartbreak, Kate wanted to give up the theater. The chance came in her mother's real estate office. A prospect wished to swap his central Oregon homestead for Seattle property. Kate grabbed at the offer, sight unseen, a mile northeast of Brothers. There was a flimsy one-room shack and a rickety shed described as the "barn." The place hadn't any well; a man hauled water for fifty cents a barrel three times weekly. In this setting of sagebrush, dust, jackrabbits and rattlesnakes, the celebrated Yukon Queen settled to prove up her claim, after spending a relaxing summer with the George Millicans of her Yukon days. Millican helped her get started and loaned her a horse.

On the High Desert, Kate was a strange sight indeed, grubbing sagebrush and rocks, and watering her desert daisies, in her bright silk dancehall gowns and flashing jewelry. She once commented that the holes about her place "aren't the tracks of prehistoric bobcats; I made'-'em with my dancing slippers."

Folks thought it strange that she'd withdrawn from the theatrical bright lights to this isolated setting. But she came to love it, especially the sunsets. Decades later, she would still return to her homestead to camp and watch the sun go down.

There was plenty of gossip about her; all were curious about this Belle of Dawson who rated as the Toast of the North. She was a charmer, always willing to entertain at dances and social happenings, and was a first-class yarn spinner. But wives felt they had to keep a tight tether on their husbands. Kate was the friendly type who encouraged the boys to drop around for coffee. Legend held that many did, that the trail to Kate's homestead was well-worn. Unlike many of her colleagues of the wild Dawson and Nome dancehalls, Kate never tried to hide her past. Instead, she capitalized on her career with what became eventually; a surge of newspaper features, magazine articles and personal appearances lasting until her dying day.

Among the cowboys who dropped around, was young Floyd Warner from the big Warner Ranch. Kate fell hard; a couple of weeks past her 39th birthday, the lovers raced on horse-

Alexander Pantages, a Greek waiter in Dawson, built a highly successful theatrical chain throughout the West. Most every city of size had its Pantages Theater. He broke with Kate, who had grubstaked him. She sued him for breech of promise and later showed up at his trial for rape in Los Angeles, but refused to testify.

In her $1,500 Paris gown, Klondike Kate created a sensation on Christmas Eve in Dawson. Sourdoughs never forgot her, proclaimed her "Queen of the Yukon."

After Kate left the Yukon, she launched a chain of theaters with her boyfriend-lover Alexander Pantages. She claimed her money from Dawson started the chain, one of the nation's largest. For awhile she teamed with Arthur Searles in a very popular "messenger boy" routine.

back into Prineville to tie the knot. But it didn't last. They fought constantly, and at times, Kate stayed alone on her place while Floyd worked his own claim on the Low Desert. When Floyd returned from the service after World War I, the pair ran a small restaurant in Prineville, living overhead. But Kate was still too freewheeling for Floyd. Eventually they divorced, Floyd moving across the Cascades to get away from her. As with Pantages, Kate had a vengeful streak and the sheriff warned Floyd that she would put him in jail for rustling if she could.

Postwar times were tough for Kate, a constant struggle to exist. She was no longer young and was unable to dance professionally since cracking a kneecap falling from a wagon. She worked in dingy cafes and logging camps, and even at scrubbing floors, barely able to make ends meet. All the while during the Roaring Twenties, Pantages' theatrical empire was growing, along with his wealth and power. He built a string of theaters in the West. Everywhere Kate went, the name "Pantages" glared back at her from the glittering marquees. She might have been his wife, she still loved him (she said) and wore the ring he gave her. He would remember the good times and help her, for Yukoners stuck together in the Code of the North.

Traveling to Los Angeles, Kate appeared at the door of his great mansion. Pantages received her coldly and gave her six dollars. Kate was shocked, her pride hurt. Again she fled back to central Oregon, this time taking up residence in Bend, where her rustic home still stands on Franklin Street. But characteristically, Kate would have the last word. When in 1929 Pantages was charged with raping a young girl, the trial became a national scandal. Kate sat day after day at the trial, but refused to testify against her former lover. Instead, she gave her entire story to the delighted press, therefore embarrassing Pantages and his family, and surely not helping his image. Bend residents were aghast at her audacity, for they never fully understood the strange woman living among them.

In Bend she was called Aunt Kate, a name that pleased her. She was controversial, beloved by some, amusing to many, and pointedly disliked by others who called her "our destitute prostitute." She was a do-gooder who too often interfered in local affairs, fed down-and-outers in the hobo jungles, fearlessly tended the sick during a ravaging influenza epidemic, counciled young girls on

(Above) Klondike Kate was Central Oregon's first rockhound. She was fascinated by the beautiful and ornate stones, which she began gathering while on the High Desert and continued after moving to Bend.

(Right) Much of Kate's rock collection went into this unique fireplace and chimney, still standing at her rustic home on Franklin Street. Note the thundereggs. On terms with Bend firemen, much to the consternation of the "good ladies of the town," Kate got the fire laddies to build her chimney. She was the firemen's first, and for years, their only "auxiliary."

(Bottom) Bend, which was also called "Farewell Bend" was a roaring frontier-style village when Klondike Kate first arrived. Impromtu horse racing was one form of recreation. Kate Rockwell settled on the High Desert near Brothers, as did many other Klondikers.

At 71, Kate "eloped" with W. A. Van Duren, a Bend bookkeeper who was living in her home. The marriage at Vancouver, Washington, in 1948, prompted international headlines proclaiming that the Queen of the Yukon was still going strong. Johnny Matson had been dead two years.

The gaysome Kate was caught sipping a soda in a Portland restaurant during one of her occasional trips there. She is still wearing the Pantages ring. Kate and Van Duren finally left Bend to live in the mid-Willamette Valley. Periodic trips were made to Central Oregon to watch sunsets on the desert where her cabin stood. Her ashes were scattered there.

their tragic love affairs. Even ministers came calling "to chat with good Aunt Kate for awhile," for she had a candid view of life. She was generous to a fault, parting with her last nickel to help another, especially a Yukon sourdough. She had a heart of gold, they said, and while she always appeared broke, she managed to increase her property holdings to several rentals; and she has a wealth of friends along the Pacific Slope and in Canada and Alaska, to where she occasionally traveled.

Kate lived in the past; she never released her hold on the turn of the century in her style of dress, her talk or her songs. Her nugget necklace and gold dust earrings were a part of her. Given to exaggeration, she loved to reminisce while rolling her own cigarettes, often with one hand. She was blunt and outspoken, fighting with her neighbors, erecting a spike fence on her property, smack against their kitchen windows. Yet she had lots of bounce, a trim figure and legs of a dancer, causing one Bend newspaperman to comment that "she was the best dancer I ever danced with; she certainly knew her business." A familiar figure on downtown streets, Kate begged vegetables and meat for her Mulligan stew to feed the hungry, then taking time to visit a local record

shop where she would sit in a booth for hours, playing the old songs.

Her growing rock collection was begun during her High Desert days. In her battered car, she ranged over the desert, bringing back jasper, agates, thundereggs, and other semiprecious stones. The weight of her collection was several tons. She began sorting this accumulation for a massive fireplace in her rustic home, its facing, thundereggs and other polished stones. Her friends in the volunteer fire department helped build it, for Kate had a way to get things done. With the leftovers, Kate built a fountain near the firehall and a small shrine on the grounds of St. Charles Hospital across the street. She also presented Bend with a sizable petrified stump placed in the city's park along the Deschutes River.

One of Kate's most noteworthy projects, which irritated the good women of Bend, was her relationship with the volunteer fire department. Her home was little more than a block from the stationhouse. Fighting fires at night in winter, with the temperature well below freezing, was a tough job, but somebody had to do it. And lately there had been a rash of blazes. One night as some 30 firemen tried controlling a particularly stubborn blaze, Kate's wheezing jalopy banged

up beside the fire truck.

"Come on, boys," Kate yelled in her throaty voice, "the coffee's on." The surprised and grateful volunteers were quickly sipping the steaming liquid and warming stiff fingers on the cups. Kate won their hearts, for nobody else had ever thought of it. From that day, Kate was a familiar figure, indeed a tradition, at every major fire.

"And sometimes," recalled one old-timer, "she'd slip us a snort from the bottle kept in her car." Prohibition didn't bother Aunt Kate.

Emulating San Francisco's Firebelle Lillie, Klondike Kate was the department's one-gal auxiliary. She gave the firemen gifts — jars of preserves and jellies, a Memory Lane tablecloth for their annual banquet, a small handsomely framed gold pan and nuggets from the Yukon, also a huge black bear rug . . . and in turn the boys made her a honorary member, with a card she carried with pride, and allowed her to ride on the fire truck during local parades.

Kate loved publicity and was determined to perpetuate the legend of the Belle of Dawson. When sourdough Johnny Maston, still living in the wilds out of Dawson, saw her picture in a Los Angeles newspaper, he wrote to Kate. He well remembered seeing her dance on Christmas Eve in Dawson when she wore lighted candles for a crown. He'd fallen in love with her that night, and never forgot her. The strange romance of Johnny and Kate is one of the Northland's cherished legends and a natural for Kate. Their marriage, in 1933 in Vancouver, British Columbia, made headlines across the land, first announced in Kate's hometown newspaper.

Johnny returned to his Klondike claim, and Kate to Bend, reaping a harvest of interviews along the way. They rendezvoused each year after the spring breakup in Dawson or Vancouver. But Matson never got to Bend, although Kate never failed to mention him and their fairytale love affair in her interviews, including a grandiose "my life story" by Bend writer Paul Hosmer which ran for a month in the Sunday magazine section of **The Oregonian.**

After Johnny died, Kate romped to the alter again, this time at Vancouver, Washington, with W.L. Van Duren, an accountant who'd been living in her house for years. This time the couple, both 71, were married in the county courthouse "for time is of the essence." Quipped Kate: "It's April Fool's Day. It's Leap Year, and besides, at my age, I don't think I'll get another chance. I was the Flower of the North, but the petals are falling fast, honey."

Soon after, Van Duren and his bride left Bend to move across the Cascades, living at Jefferson and then Sweet Home where she died in 1957 at age 80. Her remains were cremated, the ashes scattered near her desert homestead. One admirer, hearing she'd reached the end of the trail as the last of the Old West's dancehall girls, commented:

"She was quite a gal!"

It might well have been her epitaph.

Kate had red-gold hair and a fetching smile when she enticed the sourdoughs in Dawson. Kate never tried to hide the fact that she was a dance-hall girl in the wild camp, and boasted and capitalized upon it throughout her long life.

The Winning Candidate

by Alfred Powers

Motorists along the Old Oregon Trail — U.S. Highway 30 — will notice a viewpoint between Hood River and The Dalles, Oregon. This looks down upon Memaloose Island, ancient burial place of the Indians, out in the broad and swift Columbia. The only grave there now is that of a white man — Victor Trevitt — and his granite monument rises from the highest point of the island.

"I have but one wish after I die," he said, "to be laid away on Memaloose Island with the Indians. In the resurrection I will take my chances with them."

His desire was carried out in 1883 but has recently been nullified in a way he never imagined. The Indians with whom he thought he would await the eternal morning have all been taken away. Their moldering bones were removed in great quantities, because the backwater of Bonneville Dam would inundate the lower places where they were buried.

He was a saloon keeper in The Dalles. In 1861, he ran for mayor of that town.

His opponent was J. B. Wentworth, a Southerner who was president of a bank, a church member, with broad, liquid speech and with inviolable respect for the manners and actions of a gentleman.

The polls opened at eight in the morning. At nine, when he could be sure there would be a crowd to observe his action and to be influenced by it, J. B. Wentworth appeared. It was expected that the election would be close and the crowd was much interested in how he would cast his ballot, to protect his chances on the one hand and to preserve his reputation as a gentleman on the other. Everybody knew that underneath his gracious manners was much shrewdness but they also knew that he would contrive to keep whatever he did from being any blemish on his fastidious honor.

Victor Trevitt was on hand and had been there for half an hour. Although some of his adherents and all those he knew were opposed to him, looked at him in a way to show they wondered why he did not go ahead and vote, but he made no move to cast his ballot. Such was the situation still when J. B. Wentworth appeared, immaculately dressed, buoyant in mood, and charmingly cordial to supporters and well-known nonsupporters alike.

Some of Trevitt's friends saw that he looked questioningly at a particular henchman and that the latter nodded a negative. They saw, or thought they saw, a shadow of disappointment on the Wentworth countenance at this. Victor Trevitt had outsmarted him by putting the burden of proof of the first candidate vote on him. This significant interchange of looks took but a minute. Not long enough for the main crowd to note any Wentworth hesitancy.

The voting was not by Australian ballot but was oral and public at that place and time.

J. B. Wentworth approached the chairman. "I wish to cast my vote for mayoh, suh. I am a gentleman, as you all know, a gentleman above all else. I cast my ballot for my friend and honorable opponent, Victah Trevitt."

There was general applause at this. Some of Trevitt's friends didn't like it because this might win over some of those on the border line. Maybe Trevitt should have voted for Wentworth first. He would have to do so now and doing it after Wentworth would bring him no credit.

The Wentworth supporters looked at Trevitt, and even Wentworth looked at him, as if this were the time for him to reciprocate. But he made no move to vote. He merely bowed to Wentworth and said, "I thank you, sir. You have set a good example for others to follow."

Wentworth stood around for a little while, slightly ill at ease for all his good breeding, and then left. Shortly thereafter Victor Trevitt also left. "I shall vote later in the day," he said to the chairman, "if it is agreeable to you." He went to his saloon.

The polls closed at eight in the evening. By seven-thirty everybody had voted except Victor Trevitt. And the vote was a tie — 327 for J. B. Wentworth and 327 for Victor Trevitt.

The Trevitt voters were downcast. This was the equivalent of Wentworth's victory. After what has happened, there was only one way for Trevitt to vote and he was definitely the only one left. Under the circumstances, it would be an equally unheard of procedure for him to fail to vote, to let the tie stand, and to require another election.

At seven-forty-five Victor Trevitt left his saloon and went to the poling place. A crowd had remained there for this final and dramatic ballot. Others, seeing him come out of his building, followed him.

There was only one thing for him to do, but it would be interesting to see how he did it. J. B. Wentworth was already there and was being congratulated by many.

Victor Trevitt came in. He walked up to Wentworth and shook hands. "I am honored, sir," he said, "to have you present at the casting of my vote."

En route to the chairman, he cheerfully greeted his friends. "Sir," he addressed the official, "I am now ready to cast my ballot for mayor. This morning the Honorable J. B. Wentworth, my worthy opponent, paid me the great tribute of voting for me . . ."

"All over but the shouting," said one Trevitt supporter to another in the far end of the room. "Trevitt's going to vote for that old bag of wind and make a pretty speech about it to boot."

"He's going to be a good sport about it," said a Wentworth supporter to another at the edge of the crowd. "He knows where his bread's buttered. He will want the mayor to go easy on his saloon license."

" . . . the Honorable J. B. Wentworth is a gentleman," continued Victor Trevitt, "and could not do otherwise, as he told you. Now, I am not a gentleman, as you all know, but only a saloon keeper, a friend of the Indians, and your humble friend. I simply feel it is my duty as it is the duty of every citizen to vote for the one I consider the better candidate — and in doing so I am only following in the action of my honorable opponent."

"Now, The Dalles has a large population of Indians. It is the original home of the Wascos and many Klickitats cross the Columbia River to trade and visit, to make the town one of the largest Indian gathering places on the river.

"I am the best friend they have, almost their only white friend. These people are not allowed to vote. If they were allowed to, I think you will agree that all of them would have voted for me. In my decision I am simply recognizing their right to vote. Either my honorable opponent or I would probably make satisfactory mayor of the whites, but I am voting for the one who would also be a mayor for the Indians. Therefore, Mr. Chairman, I cast my vote for Victor Trevitt."

Said the chairman, "Gentlemen, this concludes the balloting. Victor Trevitt has been elected mayor of The Dalles."

Bethenia Owens: Post-Mortem Pioneer

By Robert W. Pelton

It was 1878 when Bethenia Owens, divorcee and mother of a bright son, decided to complete her medical education at the Jefferson Medical Center in Philadelphia. She was refused entrance because she was a woman! So the spirited lady then applied at the University of Michigan, a much more farsighted institution, and was accepted. And her son? He left for the Golden State to begin his own medical career.

But this was not the real beginning of Bethenia's story of unlimited courage and tenacity. 1872 marked the start of world-wide fame and even notariety for the pretty woman in her early thirties. She had been working on a degree in medicine at the Philadelphia Eclectic College, a visionary

school in its day, and one of the few to allow females through its entrance. After all, women belonged in the home, didn't need higher education, and were designed only to bear children!

Roseburg, Oregon, a quiet little pioneer community proved to be the historial setting for Bethenia's contribution to women's emancipation and medicine. Roseburg's leading doctor was the unknowing catalyst — he had been responsible for seeing that Bethenia was invited to an autopsy. Yes, old Doc Barnes had always believed that, "women have no place being present at an autopsy." And this particular autopsy was to be performed on of all things, a man!

On the day of the autopsy, Bethenia

hurried along a dusty country road leading to an old ramshackle barn outside of town. The whole community was bubbling with excitement and anticipation. It was a typical hot summery day in Roseburg. Men had dropped their hoes and tied the mules. Women left meals to burn on the stove and gathered on the wooden sidewalks in town. There they whispered and chuckled about the impulsive young woman who was about to be humiliated by old Doc Barnes.

Joe Marcy, an alcoholic drifter and town pauper, had died! Autopsies at this time in history, were somewhat public events attended only by men. They were important social happenings which were ghoulish, yet exciting to witness. Over sixty men

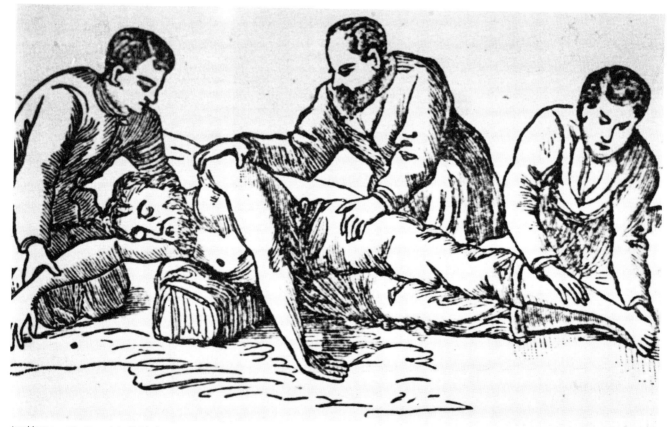

Joe Marcy — pauper and derilict, being prepared for the autopsy.

Doc stared contemptuously at Bethenia, as her pretty eyes held his gaze. Her face was flushed with excitement, or was it from the strain and pressure placed upon her shoulders? He shouted as he peered around at the men present, "God knows, a woman doesn't belong here. Not when I'm doing an autopsy on a man! Who does she think she is? Well, boys, don't worry, she'll never last through this! She'll faint for sure!"

Bethenia retained her composure and responded quietly, "I don't see that this is any different than a man performing an autopsy on a woman."

The stillness was nerve-wracking as Bethenia looked around the room. Doctor Barnes sarcastically noted that this man's death involved a part of his anatomy embarrassing to any upstanding Christian woman. Bethenia paled, then blushed. But she wouldn't back down. Her response was firm, "I don't understand how this can be so different. All segments of the human body are the same to a medical doctor."

"Well, then," said Doc Barnes sarcastically, "you perform this autopsy. Do it if you think you can!"

A small black bag of medical instruments was suddenly handed to Bethenia. The men in attendance were frightfully uneasy at this moment. Would this young upstart really do the job? Does she really have the nerve? Such audacity!

And Bethenia? Here, finally, was her grand opportunity. She could now put to rest the derision heaped upon her for years since she decided to become a doctor. But the odors emitting from the body under the blanket almost made her vomit. And the smells coming from the sweaty men in the packed barn didn't help much. The hatred felt in the community wasn't exactly a source of inner security.

Could this youthful girl in a flowery summer dress meet the challenge? After all, her medical schooling was not at all like doing the real thing. **Gray's Anatomy** had been perused and memorized for untold hours. All she really knew was what she had learned from drawings, charts and diagrams — not from actual on-the-job experience. Would it be sufficient? Only a few other American women had already become doctors, and not one had done surgery of any type.

Bethenia took a deep breath and carefully turned up the sleeves of her dress. She wore no gloves as these were unheard of in medicine at this period of history. Her bare hands would have to actually touch the cold body under the filthy blanket. She rolled back the covering and began

Doc Barnes — who planned to humiliate Dr. Owens during her first autopsy.

showed up for Marcy's "cutting." No one in Roseburg believed that Bethenia, although invited, would ever dare appear. But indeed she did, head held high and smiling.

"Some nerve!" whispered the other women in Roseburg. "How dare she do this! Wait 'till she takes a look at old Marcy. Just wait. He's been dead now for over two days. She'll come running soon as she sees his body."

"Bethenia will get sick. She'll get what she deserves."

"Her and her dumb ideas about women being doctors! Just watch! She'll stop this silly thinking after this!"

"Who does she think she is. Don't she know her place?"

None of the laughter and insults bothered Bethenia. If it did, she refused to let anyone know how she felt. But she did fear the barbs expected from the men. She approached the unpainted barn and could hear the men boisterously cursing and joking about the "woman who was going to see something she shouldn't." Undaunted, yet a little nervous, Bethenia reached the barn door and cautiously opened it. Everyone became quiet when she walked inside — no man would look her in the eyes.

The fun was about to begin. Doc Barnes was happy. He was about to make a fool of this "reckless woman." He was more than a little astounded when Bethenia caught his glance, put out her hand and said: "Doctor Barnes, I want to thank you for your kind invitation. It is certainly an honor to work with you. I look for-her work in earnest, trying not to pay any attention to those around her. The crowd in the barn became silent and edged nearer to get a better look at what was taking place.

Autopsies were normally performed on the frontier as a means to fulfill a craving for excitement. Bethenia was aware of this, yet she also realized the importance of the task. Her undertaking of the autopsy only added to the feverish excitement of the event. She worked quietly and efficiently and made the initial cut with the steady knife. A Y-shaped incision was quickly done and she reached inside in an effort to locate some of the internal reasons for the man's death. She was aware that only readily obvious conclusions could be reached, and she also realized how careful she must be in stating her findings to Doctor Barnes, especially in the presence of such a hostile group of spectators.

Bethenia finished her observations and quietly told Barnes what she

Bethenia Owens, over a fifty year period, was successful in penetrating the shrouds of ignorance, superstition, and prejudice concerning women in America.

She overcame a multitude of taboos in her crusade to free the female population from man-imposed rules.

concluded. She then proceeded to stitch up the body properly and prepare it for burial. Doctor Barnes was angry but silent. The woman was quite right! He grudgingly stepped back and said nothing as she washed her hands in cold water, dried them on the dirty blanket, and walked out of the barn. A few of the men cheered the brave lady as she left, but even this quickly stopped when others gave them unapproving stares.

No one, even the old doctor, had attempted to criticize Bethenia's autopsy. Her conclusions were admirably correct, and the procedures she followed were letter perfect. But, no matter how perfect Bethenia's handiwork, she was obviously before her time. The town women ignored her as she walked by on her way back home. Most silently rocked and stared when she passed. One simply couldn't restrain herself any longer and screamed: "Bethenia Owens! You have disgraced all of us! Why don't you leave town. We don't need you here!"

This started a tirade of catcalls and insulting remarks: "Shame! Shame! Shame!" "Go away Bethenia Owens! Leave town, leave town." "Your family is disgraced Owens!" "You're not wanted around here!" And the children, almost all of them, following the example set by their parents, began to boo.

Bethenia was shaken although she had expected such a mass reaction. The hatred and despise numbed her entire being — she looked pale and drawn. She knew she was a medical pioneer and the first female to ever perform surgery, to use a scalpel, to do an autopsy. But she was too worn out to now care. All she wanted to do was get to her home, lock the doors and windows, pull the drapes, and be left alone. She also realized that Roseburg, Oregon, was not the place for her to begin a thriving medical practice.

Bethenia left Roseburg and relocated in Portland where she opened for business. She hung her shingle out and advertised as a "Bath Doctor," the only medical practice allowed women in those days. She could legally give medical baths to patients, but nothing else under fear of prosecution. Her practice flourished and she saved her money. By 1878 she was ready to complete her medical training and eventually moved to Michigan to attend the University of Michigan. Two years later her degree was awarded and she left for Chicago where she became an intern — the only woman intern in existence there! Later she traveled and studied in Europe, sitting in on the operations of the world's foremost surgeons.

Eventually returning to Oregon, Bethenia finally had her complete medical practice. She continued until in her eighties and for over 50 of those long productive years, she fought for women's equality in medicine, and brought forth many medical and health ideas then thought to be revolutionary by her peers. Bethenia challenged old ideas — she campaigned against women wearing harsh, tight-fitting corsets. These she felt were harmful to women's health. She spoke out against women never being seen hatless in public. She was against women riding a horse in the accepted sidesaddle manner. She promoted women's athletics, stressing the importance of conditioning the muscles, although such athletics were considered to be only for men.

Harvard's president, Charles W. Eliot, was one of Bethenia's chief critics. He challenged her views in the belief that a woman's place was to simply bear children. Eliot was honestly afraid that higher education for women would damage their ability to conceive and give birth. He felt the same way about sports and outdoor activities, especially exercise — **and this was the president of Harvard!** But Bethenia, herself, was educated and highly athletic. She remarried at 44 and subsequently gave birth to another child at age 47. Thus she proved him wrong!

For a full fifteen years, Bethenia doggedly fought with the legislators of Oregon over the passing of a new law. She wanted medical exams for everyone applying for a marriage license. The new law was finally passed and signed by Oregon's governor in 1922. As a result, Bethina Owens Adair became an international celebrity. Eugenics resultingly became a subject which could be discussed in public. **The Portland Journal** editorialized: "A personal triumph for Dr. Owens-Adair."

Bethenia Owens, later Adair, over a fifty year period, was successful in penetrating through the shrouds of ignorance, superstition and prejudice concerning women in America. She overcame a multitude of taboos in her crusade to free the female population from man-imposed rules. By her own example, by lectures throughout the nation, and in daily conversations, she finally won her lifelong battle against medieval beliefs.

Her courage was unlimited. Her determination unbelievable. Her ability unchallenged. The ordeal in the ramshackle barn in Roseburg had been the catalyst. No obstacle in her path was too big to overcome. She dared, against all odds, to be one of America's truly heroic medical pioneers!

The Whitman Mission – Cradle of Northwest History

By Vernon Selde

The signing of the Louisiana Purchase almost doubled the size of the United States. While pleased with their apparent bargain, the fledgling American Government was mystified and concerned with the extent of the northern and western boundaries of this vast uncharted wilderness. Speculation and rumors ran wild about the riches and dangers that this huge mass of deserts, mountains and forests might contain. Little was known about the climate, soil fertility or native populations here. The Lewis and Clark Expedition was hastily organized to find out in 1804.

After one year of mapping the northern Rockies, the expedition continued west, seeking the rumored "River of the West" and mysterious "Oregon". They found both — and the western edge of the continent along the heavily forested Pacific shore. For the first time, an accurate map could be made of the continent. Much of the mystery was erased, and a strong claim was established for the United States when the contingent returned to the Nation's capital in 1806 — a claim soon to be contested by Russia, Spain and Great Britain.

By 1818, however, the active claimants to "Oregon" were reduced to just the United States and Great Britain, who in that year signed a "Joint Occupancy Treaty", setting the stage for a precarious ownership struggle that was to last for another 30 years.

Subsequent contacts between the white man and the native Indians in this remote "Oregon" wilderness soon led to demands by the Indians not only for the white man's goods and medicine, but also for the "black robes", as the Indians referred to the Catholic priests. Word of this request by the Indians for priests soon reached the American Board of Foreign Missions of the Presbyterian Church in Boston, and from a number of volunteers they selected several couples including Dr. Marcus Whitman and his wife, Narcissa. Then Dr. Whitman, who was not only a minister of the gospel, but a trained doctor of medicine, was named to head this group of missionaries soon to depart for far away mysterious "Oregon".

After accumulating horses, wagons, livestock, food and other items considered essential to their survival, the Whitmans and another couple, the Spauldings, left St. Louis overland in the spring of 1836 for their new home in the wilderness. Up to now, only rugged mountain men had traveled this way, and they had gone only as far as the Rocky Mountains. They were warned that they might perish.

To get to their destination, they had to travel over 2000 miles of uncharted, barren, rocky and dusty prairie, snow clogged mountains, swift rivers and rugged canyons. Many flood-swollen river crossings lay ahead. There were no signs to point the way and few landmarks to guide them. They were accompanied only by a few American Fur Company men, going only as far as the Rocky Mountains.

No white woman had traveled this route before. If they survived, they would be the first white women in the vast wilderness of Old Oregon. Their example was to become a beacon for many other white females who were to follow the same route in a few years.

After surviving numerous incidents concerning lack of proper food and water, unfriendly natives, floods, illness and other perils, the missionaries arrived on July 4, 1836 at South Pass, considered about one-half the distance. By this time much of their furniture, clothing and other items had been discarded along the trail in an effort to lighten the load and speed up the travel. (This proved to be the first of thousands of items that were to be discarded on this famous trail over the next 30 years, making it a "litterbug" trail 2000 miles long.) Modern highways that now parallel this famous trail have signs to mark their way. Pioneers of the Oregon Trail that followed had only wagon ruts and the discarded personal items of the emigrants (and the Whitmans) that traveled this route before them to guide their way.

Weeks later at the Hudson's Bay fur trading post of Fort Hall, still some 600 miles from their final destination, they were advised to abandon their wagons, which they did. Here all gear that could not be carried on horseback was abandoned or sold, the rest of the trail being considered too dangerous, slow and impractical for the use of wagons.

On September 1 they caught sight of the Hudson's Bay Post of Fort Walla Walla ahead, on the arid, treeless shore of the mighty Columbia River. It was reported that they were so excited that in galloping the last mile they forgot the soreness and weariness of this long and perilous journey.

It was here at Fort Walla Walla that the Whitmans first saw and were impressed by the robust gardens containing a variety of vegetables that had been planted by the Hudson's Bay personnel there. They were even more impressed by the extensive orchards they saw growing at Vancouver while visiting there after a 200 mile journey by boat down the mighty Columbia River, the week following their arrival at Fort Walla Walla. It was here that they were cordially greeted and entertained by the Hudson's Bay Company superintendent, Dr. McLoughlin, called the "Great White Eagle" by the Indians — a man who was to become an important influence and benefactor to the Whitmans during the next 11 years of their lives.

Following the advice of Dr. McLoughlin and others, the Whitmans decided to establish their mission some 25 miles upstream on the Walla Walla River at a sight the Indians called "Waiilaptu", or "the place of the people of the rye grass", named for the tall rye grass which grew wild at this site then, as it does now.

Shortly, with the enthusiastic permission of leaders of the Cayuse Tribe who had camps nearby, and with the help of fellow emigrants, the Whitmans staked out some 300 acres of fertile land along the Walla Walla River. With tools purchased from Hudson's Bay Company, foundations for a house 30 feet by 36 feet were excavated and adobe brick consisting of straw and mud, formed and dried in the sun, for later use in wall construction. By the middle of October a good start had been made on this first mission house.

Mission Construction

Work on the new house was slow, due to lack of dependable, experienced and productive labor. All boards had to be sawed by hand from cottonwood trees found growing along the river banks. This was done using whipsaws about 6 feet long, with one man on the lower end in a pit and the top man on top of the log being sawed. It soon became obvious that the house would not be completed before winter set in, so construction efforts were concentrated on the

building of a lean-to along the west wall of the uncompleted new house. It was 36 feet long by 12 feet wide, with a large adobe fireplace along the center of the west wall. The roof consisted of poles covered with abundant native rye grass, on which about 6 inches of sod was placed to shed snow and rain.

With the snowline low in the nearby Blue Mountains, Mrs. Whitman, now 6 months pregnant, moved into her first new home, traveling the 25 miles on horseback from Fort Walla Walla where she had been a guest of the Hudson's Bay Company. In spite of the fact that her house had only blankets where windows and doors were to be, excerpts from letters to her mother revealed her delight with this humble abode. The missing windows were not in place until February 18, 1837 — on December 25, 18 inches of snow fell and remained on the ground well into February. So began the first year at the Whitman Mission.

In letters to relatives she boasted of her new found comforts, and described her 3 homemade chairs and bedstead, and expressed a wish "to soon have a barrel to pound her clothes in for washing". The chair she described as "deer skin bottoms woven as the fancy chair in the States" were made from crude cottonwood logs, as was most of the furniture that was built later. It was in this humble abode that the first child to be born of white American parents in the vast wilderness was born, when on March 14, 1837 the pioneering Whitmans became the proud parents of a baby girl, named Alice Clarissa, fair and blonde like her mother.

Food Supplies

Letters by the Whitmans show they were dependent upon both the Indians and the Hudson's Bay Company for food. In addition to 9 wild horses furnished by the Indians for food (for which goods were traded), potatoes, corn, butter, flour, pork and some venison was purchased from Hudson's Bay Company. Their dependence on others for food was gradually eased as salmon obtained from nearby rivers and produce from their gardens became available. Later, as more acres were irrigated, planted and cultivated here, food was made available to destitute white emigrants and native Indians alike. In one year, the Whitman's agricultural efforts, using seeds and tools obtained from Hudson's Bay Company, were so successful as to supply all of the mission's food needs except for beef.

Not surprisingly, visiting Indians were quick to note and appreciate the

produce from the Whitman gardens. Soon peas, corn and potatoes set aside for a seed supply for the Indians became a large part of the production from the Mission gardens. However, lack of sufficient plows, hoes and other tools, along with the nomadic habits of these natives, slowed development of serious gardening efforts on their part. But by 1840, with the arrival of the long-ordered and much-needed tools, native gardens soon became numerous in areas near the mission.

While success was had in breaking Indian ponies for the plow, mules and oxen from the Whitman herd and animals procured from Hudson's Bay did most of the plowing during these first years. Production of grains and the demand for tools was assisted by the construction of a grist mill and blacksmith shop at the Mission. In a short time the grist mill was grinding flour for both the Mission and native farmers who hauled their grain to the mill site by horseback or cart.

By using seeds and sprouts from fruit trees found growing at Fort Vancouver, Whitman established a small orchard, which he watered by a ditch to the Walla Walla River. This pioneering venture proved to be the first irrigation system in Oregon, a prelude to the millions of acres that were brought under irrigation in the next 100 years (what we see today) in this area.

With the arrival of additional missionaries in 1838 and the demand for medical, agricultural and gospel services by the Indians, Dr. Whitman became a very busy man. Not only were the Waiilatpu Mission buildings expanded, but new missions at Lapwai and Tshim-a kain, several hundred miles to the north, were built and staffed. To service these missions it was necessary for Whitman to travel cross-country on horseback, a slow, grueling trip requiring the fording of large, cold and swift rivers. The way was marked only by Indian trails that wound in and out among the treeless hills and arid, rocky gullies that scarred the landscape. This also put a great burden on Mrs. Whitman, who was required to feed and shelter numerous visitors, settlers and Indians alike. It became the habit of passing emigrant trains to leave sick and orphaned children as well as ill adults at the Mission until they recovered and were found a permanent home. Some of these orphans were adopted by the Whitmans.

In 1839, tragedy in the form of the accidental drowning of 2 year old Alice Whitman in the nearby Walla Walla River struck the Whitmans. This blow, while severe, seemed only to make these brave pioneers more determined than ever to accomplish their service to emigrants and residents of the surrounding countryside.

To accommodate the large number of visitors and settlers at Waiilatpu, a large T-shaped building was built of adobe bricks and timber. It was divided into a number of rooms including a schoolroom, kitchen, sitting room, bedrooms and the ever-busy Indian room. This was used to house visiting natives and was built to reduce the habits of Indians entering into any and all rooms of the Mission, without knocking, any time of day or night. Although this may have reduced the problem, it remained a major one.

Plagued by bickering among his fellow missionaries, and trouble with ill and discontented Indians who often threatened him with bodily harm, Whitman received shocking news in the form of a letter from the Board of Foreign Missions in February of 1842. The bad news — his mission at Waiilatpu was to be closed and his missionaries were to be terminated!

After several discussions with his fellow missionaries, it was decided he would return east on horseback to state his case, not only to the Board of Foreign Missions but also to the President of the United States. Starting in October, with only 2 horses and a companion, he struck out on his historic, long, and desperate mid-winter journey of almost 6 months for the nation's capital. The journey was made more difficult by a 1000 mile detour made because of Indian problems at South Pass on the Oregon Trail. During this detour he became lost, almost starved, and suffered severely from frostbite.

His arrival at the nation's capital received much publicity, and through friends he was able to talk at length with President Tyler, members of his Cabinet and other persons involved in government. His arguments were so persuasive that he was able to convince a wavering President and Congress to vote considerable government commitment to protection by troops to and in the vast and disputed territory of Oregon. Immigration overland to Oregon, which had been ignored by the Federal government, was to be encouraged and troops sent to protect the travelers.

Meetings with newspaper editors and Whitman produced more publicity and support not only for the Whitman Mission, but for the United States' claim to this vast territory. Editor Horace Greeley and others

printed Whitman's tantalizing descriptions of his agricultural successes along with the timber, water, fish and potential mineral wealth available to those willing to emigrate, live and work in this yet untamed territory. Even the Board of Foreign Missions was convinced of the value of the Whitman Mission, and cancelled the order for closing the Mission. New and greater support was promised.

In his travels about the New England states, Whitman was besieged by questions about this far away land by persons interested in establishing homes there. Many insisted on returning with him on his scheduled return trip that spring (1843). Knowing that to accompany this caravan west would delay his arrival at Wailatpu by several months, he was reluctant to do so, but when told that Lt. Fremont and 30 federal troops were to accompany the wagon train on their western journey, he agreed to do so.

On May 22, 1843, this great wagon train (by far the largest to date), including over 800 emigrants, 120 wagons and several thousand cattle, horses and mules, departed a site near the present Kansas City for far-off Oregon. Among them was Dr. Whitman. This historic event was to be followed by even larger wagon trains in 1844 and 1845.

Years later, when a permanent peace treaty was signed by the United States and England, giving the lion's share of what is now Washington, Oregon and Idaho to the United States, historians were to credit Whitman's historic ride as "saving Oregon for the United States."

Historians argue that had not Whitman made this historic trip, this migration to Oregon would not have occurred in time to prove to the peace treaty makers of the United States, as well as those of England, that this wagon train route was safe for the migration of both wagons and females. It also must have been obvious to all parties that these migrations were just the beginning of what were to be even larger influxes of pioneering Americans to this region, thus tipping the population balance greatly in favor of the United States. In 1848 it became Oregon Territory, U.S.A.

When members of this great 1843 wagon train reached Waiilatpu in late October, many were short on food, clothing and other critical supplies, even those necessary for the short trip down the river to Fort Vancouver. Whitman graciously furnished their needs, even to the extent of leaving himself with short supplies. He then realized and planned accordingly for

the needs of the much larger emigrant trains of the following years.

In preparation for the housing of orphans and disabled adults of the next annual emigration, the mission buildings were enlarged and the grist mill which had been burned by Indians during his absence the year before was restored. Additional acres were plowed and planted to corn, wheat, peas and potatoes. Fences were built to protect gardens from Indian horses and cattle which roamed at will and often destroyed fields of gardens and grain alike.

As some expected, this great influx of white settlers had a great influence on the already unhappy Indians. Many resented the services made available to the emigrants by the Mission because they logically thought this meant less for them. Others were angered by whites trespassing on their lands, scaring away the game and constructing fences to restrict the movements of livestock. Finally diseases to which the white man was immune struck the Indians a devastating blow. The trouble pot began to boil!

Because Dr. Whitman was a medical doctor as well as a minister of the gospel, he felt obligated to treat all humans, but with the smallpox and measles epidemics in many local tribes, he was hard put to meet the many demands of the natives asking for his medicine. Because the Indians had very little resistance to these diseases, Whitman's chances for success were very small, and the death rate was high. The native's habits and superstitions made the chances of recovery even smaller. To make matters worse, competing native shamans and medicine men ridiculed his efforts and spread rumors of poison. The fact that few whites in the Mission became sick lent suspicion and credance to the poison theory, setting the stage for the disastrous massacre that destroyed the Mission and the lives of many of its inhabitants late in 1847. However, the destruction of the Whitmans and their Mission did not mean the end of settlement for the United States in this area. In fact, it appears to have signalled the beginning. The Whitman Mission proved to be the cradle in which modern Pacific Northwest history was born.

Little Known Tales from Oregon History

No. 25

The Sheep King of America

By David Braly

There used to be a spacious three-story mansion on a ranch in what is today Jefferson County where nobles, governors, celebrities and such magnates as Sam Hill and Edward H. Harriman were entertained. Their host was the man who was known worldwide as "the Sheep King": Jack Edwards.

Born in 1855 in Wales, John Griffith Edwards came to America in 1872. He went to Evanston, Wyoming and acquired the Circle-O cattle ranch, which he operated until he was broken by a severe winter and the raids of the Utes. He worked as an army scout until 1885 when he became a sheep raiser.

Over a period of time Jack Edwards acquired 100,000 sheep, making him the biggest sheep rancher in the country. Then cattlemen attacked him. Edwards fought them on the ranges of Colorado and Utah. But next homesteaders came in, filed on the ranges, and took the land out from under both Edwards and his enemies.

Edwards looked for new land. He wanted the best sheep ranch that he could find. The one that eventually attracted his attention was Oregon's large Hay Creek Ranch 25 miles north of Prineville.

The Hay Creek Ranch had been started in 1873 by Dr. David W. Baldwin, a practicing physician from

The Hay Creek Ranch shearing plant. During its first year in operation the plant sheared 42,000 sheep. About 500,000 pounds of wool were sold every year. Oregon Historical Society Photo.

Boston. Dr. Baldwin had bought 160 acres of land in Central Oregon and brought registered Spanish Merino sheep from Vermont, shipping them overland 1,000 miles. The doctor's Baldwin Sheep & Land Company eventually spread across several thousand acres, buying up adjoining homesteads and unused tracts nearby, and raised the first alfalfa ever grown in Oregon. It was possession of this alfalfa — 2,500 tons of which was harvested seasonally — and of free government land rich with knee-high bunch grass that allowed the ranch to prosper.

Dr. Baldwin's health failed and in 1884 he sold the company. C.A. and J.P. Van Houten, H. Loneoy, John Summerville and others were the new owners.

Jack Edwards arrived on the scene in 1898. He bought a half-interest in the company, which gave him control. He acquired almost all of the company in 1905 when he bought out the interests of his principal partners, State Sentor Charles Cartwright and J.P. Van Houten.

Once again, Jack Edwards became the sheep king of America. He expanded the Hay Creek Ranch to cover 27,000 acres of deeded land. However, this wasn't the entire territory controlled by the ranch. Its sheep were allowed to graze freely on the open ranges of what is today Jefferson County and in parts of western Wasco and northwestern Crook counties. Other land was leased from private or public owners. Edwards set up camps at every spring in that wide area. This allowed him to build up his flocks until he had about 50,000 sheep, making his Hay Creek spread the largest sheep ranch in the United States.

Edwards did more than just acquire more land and more sheep. He was interested in cross-breeding to produce finer wool and better mutton. He was determined to make his ranch renowned for its high quality and was prepared to pay almost any price to accomplish that end.

His experiment with cross-breeding began when he purchased Rambouillet sheep from the French government and two estates in France. These three organizations had the only purebred Rambouillets in the world until Edwards began establishing his own flock. Eventually he would have 800 Rambouillets, for which he sometimes paid as much as $2,000 for each ram. This flock was the largest in the world because even the French government's flock numbered only 300.

After he brought over the Rambouillets he crossed them with the ranch's Spanish Merino and Delaines. The result was a very large sheep weighing up to 200 pounds, thick fleeced from nose to hooves, free of grease and wrinkles, and producing more wool and more mutton than other breeds. This new and reproductive breed was called the Baldwin Sheep and quickly became internationally known.

However, not all of the sheep were interbred. Edwards kept separate flocks of Spanish Merinos, Delaines and Rambouillets which were mated only with others of their own breed. This was done to keep purebred rams available for sale as breeding stock. Edwards sold these purebreds to sheep ranchers all over the United States. He also exported many of his rams to farmers in the Natal and Cape colonies of South Africa.

Edwards had a conservative sales policy for his rams and never sold ewes. He believed that his strength lay in building up large flocks of the highest quality sheep and retaining the ewes was a natural part of such a policy. The quality, incidentally, was assured because Edwards paid the highest prices for prize-winning rams and ewes at various expositions and fairs. Besides purchasing blue ribbon stock at shows in the Eastern and Midwestern U.S., Edwards bought the prize-winning sheep from the 1902

Baldwin Sheep and Land Co. Mercantile Store with wagons loaded with wool in front. Oregon Historical Society Photo. Oregon Department of Transportation Photo

Paris Exposition and other competitions in France. Cost was no object where quality was concerned.

A work force of up to 100 men cared for the sheep. Each year between 12,000 and 15,000 new ewes were bred on the ranch and these and the other sheep were carefully nurtured and raised. As far as possible, Edwards made the ranch self-sufficient. He maintained a cattle herd of 1,500 to 2,000 head annually and grew about 6,000 tons of hay annually. Despite its enormous flocks and herds, the Hay Creek Ranch almost never had to buy hay.

It became the first ranch to install a sheep-shearing plant. This plant greatly accelerated the ranch's self-sufficiency. During its first year in operation the plant sheared 42,000 sheep. After that, about 500,000 pounds of wool was sold every year by the Hay Creek Ranch. Some of the wool was taken through Prineville in large wagons; most was shipped out through Shaniko, which became the largest wool shipping station in the Pacific Northwest.

The ranch built and operated a general store at Hay Creek. Its customers were ranch employees and nearby settlers. Most of these settlers were men who took up homesteads which they proved and then sold several years later to the Baldwin Sheep & Land Company. While they were living on their homesteads they worked for the Hay Creek Ranch. Usually they worked as herders, although many also found employment in the shearing plant.

Almost everything grown on the ranch was put to use. The tops of the early alfalfa crops were cut and used in salads at the cookhouse and in the Edwards house. The ranch gardener raised a wide variety of fruits and vegetables which were consumed there and at the distant sheep camps and in the kitchens of nearby farms.

Meanwhile, in 1903, Jack Edwards married Elizabeth Justice Bell Smith of England. It was for her that he built his large house. Together they were hosts to some of the most famous people of their time, but more important they followed a policy of hospitality and generosity towards their neighbors which many ranchers of that time never attempted. When someone in the area was sick or in need, they turned to the Hay Creek Ranch for help and the help was always forthcoming. At a time when other Central Oregon ranchers were at war with homesteaders, the huge Hay Creek Ranch — which might have easily aroused their envy and hostility — was looked upon by homesteaders as a friend.

When Crook County's fierce range war between cattle and sheep ranchers broke out early in this century Edwards spoke out against the depredations and killings. However, none of the masked gunmen of the Crook County Sheep Shooting Association rode against the Hay Creek Ranch.

Edwards spent most of his time tending to ranch operations. He did speak out against the cattlemen's gunmen and against a plan to divide giant Crook County (which would also have divided his ranch). However, it was the raising and selling of sheep that absorbed his interest. It was just that, after all, for which Edwards had become internationally known. During the first decade of the new century Edwards was selling an average of about 4,000 rams annually.

But trouble arrived during those same years that were so prosperous for him. It came not from the cattlemen or the homesteaders, but from the newly-established Forest Service.

The Forest Service had the authority to set grazing allotments on government land. It was largely this power that enabled the Forest Service to stop the Crook County range war. Instead of prior grazing rights or gunpower deciding who could graze how much stock on what tracts of land, the Forest Service decided. At first it set the grazing allotment for the Hay Creek Ranch in the Blue Mountain Forest Reserve at 40,000 sheep.

Then the Forest Service began to systematically whittle down the Hay Creek Ranch's allotment. In 1906 it cut the allotment by a whopping 40 percent. Two years later it cut it by another 40 percent. Edwards fought this second cut by using all of his financial and political clout in Oregon and at the nation's capital. Finally the Forest Service was forced to modify the cut to 25 percent, which allowed the Hay Creek Ranch to graze almost 18,000 sheep on public lands.

Edwards cut back his operations to accommodate the allotment. He figured that he could still make a profit by holding his flocks to 20,000 sheep of the highest quality. He made his future plans on that basis.

Late in 1909 the Forest Service informed Edwards that the Hay Creek Ranch's allotment for 1910 was to be cut by another 30 percent. This came as a complete surprise to Edwards. He had thought that the issue of the allotments was settled. And — because he had used all of his muscle in 1908 and managed to get only a partial reduction in the cut — he didn't believe that he could successfully challenge the new cut.

In December Edwards rode to Portland, where he began making arrangements to sell the ranch. An Oregon Journal reporter talked with him at the Portland Hotel, where Edwards said that the ranch would be closed down and all of its sheep sold.

"The flocks . . . have for many years required a certain grazing area in the forest reserve," explained Edwards. "From time to time the Forestry Department has reduced this area and each time we have been compelled to cut down the size of our flocks. We are now notified by the Department that another cut has been made and this will reduce our flocks to a number much below that which we must necessarily have to run the Hay Creek breeding plant profitably . . . I mean no criticism of the Government, but the facts are as I have stated. Twelve months from the present date we expect to have our entire sheep holdings sold out."

In March 1910 the company advertised a close-out sale of its sheep flocks. The sheep could be bought individually or in small lots, F.O.B. Shaniko, properly crated. That same year Edwards sold the Hay Creek Ranch to Portland capitalist L.B. Menefree and Oregonian publisher Henry L. Pittock.

Jack Edwards moved to Portland. He built a mansion there and stayed clear of new business entanglements. His old mansion on the ranch, incidentally, burned down in 1924.

Perhaps to his surprise, the Hay Creek Ranch survived. Indeed, it thrived. In Edwards' lifetime it had several changes of ownership. Menefree and Pittock sold it to W.U. Sanderson in 1922 and he sold it in 1937 to Fred W. Wickman. It also had a new customer: Joe Stalin.

The Soviet government wanted to upgrade the quality of the sheep on the Steppes and sent experts abroad to find high quality sheep to inbreed with the Russian stock. After touring France, England and the greatest sheep ranches in America, the Russians appeared at the Hay Creek Ranch and found what they were looking for. In November 1927 two trains of 27 cars loaded with 10,000 sheep took the first leg of the journey to Russia by pulling out of the Madras railroad station.

As for Jack Edwards — former sheep king of America — he spent the rest of his days in Portland. Although he'd gotten a raw deal from Uncle Sam he didn't whine about it. He occupied his time by painting. When Edwards died, in 1945, he left $700,000 of his estate to public use.

Look what's coming up in the next

Little Known Tales from Oregon History

Volume III

Scheduled for publication in 1993

Available at Sun Publishing, 716 NE 4th Street *(behind Safeway/Andersch)*, Bend, or at local bookstores and merchants.

To order by mail send $14.00 (includes postage and handling) to:
Sun Publishing, P.O. Box 5784, Bend, OR 97708

See page 63 for information about Little Known Tales, Volume II